Learning Styles: Putting Research and Common Sense into Practice

American Association of School Administrators
1801 North Moore Street, Arlington, VA 22209

Additional copies of *Learning Styles: Putting Research and Common Sense into Practice* may be ordered from AASA Publications, 1801 North Moore Street, Arlington, Virginia 22209. Price lists and catalogs are available upon request.

Copyright © 1991, American Association of School Administrators

Library of Congress Card Catalog Number: 91-075639

ISBN: 0-87652-169-3

AASA Stock Number: 021-00314

Contents

 # Foreword

We've always known it—people learn differently. Some are better listeners. Some are more visual. Lately, we've learned that some are more "right brained" and some are more "left brained." Researcher Howard Gardner has even theorized that we have "multiple intelligences."

For more than a decade, educators have been working to apply what we know about learning styles. The research base, according to many observers, is slim. Some theories, in fact, demand even further research. Yet, teachers, administrators, and others are generally convinced there is value in expanding the appropriate use of what we know.

Many school systems are becoming even more sensitive to the learning styles of their students. Teachers and administrators are being trained. Research and theories are being applied. Most feel the effort is yielding positive results.

At the American Association of School Administrators, we thought it was time to provide an update on learning styles. In fact, our surveys have told us that education leaders wanted to know even more about the topic.

In this book, you'll find a basic review of what researchers, theorists, and educators are saying, including comments from those who have "packaged" learning styles programs.

This publication will not tell you everything you need to know to fully implement a learning styles program. However, it will provide educators and others who care about student learning with a timely update. *Learning Styles. . .Putting Research and Common Sense into Practice* is sure to raise the level of discussion about this important issue and could very well lead to improved student achievement.

Richard D. Miller
Executive Director
American Association of School Administrators

Chapter 1

Why Learning Styles?

All children can learn.

All students learn in different ways.

These two axioms provide the structure for the changes that policymakers, researchers, and many educators anticipate will transform public education. They represent a massive turnaround from the axioms that drove education reform at the beginning of the 1900s. And they require educators to use the ways individual students learn as keys to unlock great potential in every child.

Our times require a fresh look at learning styles. In the 1980s, early learning styles research piqued the interest of enough teachers, administrators and learning specialists to spur intense activity that has lingered in practice for a decade. Much of that activity has been experimental. What growth that has been experienced came more from the link between what was known at the time about learning styles and what was often passed off as common-sense, or the intuitive beliefs of educators rather than what has been substantiated and validated through research.

Recently, educators and researchers have joined their increasing interest in the nature and uses of intelligence with scientific knowledge about how the brain works. In addition, there have been numerous cumulative studies on the effects of physical, social and cultural contexts on learning. The result is a much more fertile base for understanding how children learn.

In other words, the initial interest in learning styles seemed to emphasize "styles." Pedagogy is now entering a time when the focus is more on "learning" as the interactive process between student and teacher. It is this change and the growing number of resources available to select from and to use in individualized learning approaches that this report attempts to explain.

First, however, we need to discuss in more detail why the nature of learning has become so important, and how "learning styles" research has emerged as a critical education policy issue.

Overcoming Obsolescence

The perception often gleaned from photographs of schoolrooms, showing immigrant children sitting row upon row or rural students moving about in one-room miracles of cooperative learning, is of an education system that essentially was egalitarian and open and that provided a common experience. This picture is only half true.

An elite tradition of education existed in the very early days of the country—and, according to some, persists even now. By luck of where a student lived or the family's income or through standardized measures of intelligence, some youngsters

Survey Shows Support, Raises Questions

Learning styles are very important, according to a survey of American Association of School Administrators members. More than twice as many considered learning styles "very important" as those who considered them merely "important." Less than 1 percent of the replies said they were "not important."

However, the unanimity ended there. The answers to questions about availability and quality of teacher training, use of learning styles strategies in classrooms for teacher evaluation and approaches used varied considerably and reflected the newness of the field.

How Many Teachers in Your District Use Knowledge of Learning Styles?
(universe 68 responses)

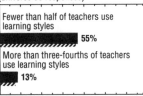

Fewer than half of teachers use learning styles — **55%**

More than three-fourths of teachers use learning styles — **13%**

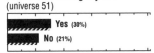

Is the Evaluation of Teachers Tied to Use of Learning Styles?
(universe 51)

Yes (30%)

No (21%)

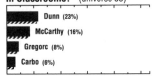

What Major Approaches Are Used In Classrooms? (universe 53)

Dunn (23%)

McCarthy (16%)

Gregorc (8%)

Carbo (6%)

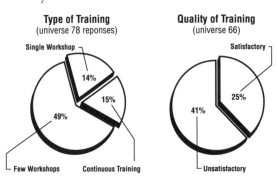

Type of Training
(universe 78 reponses)

Single Workshop — 14%
15%
49%
Few Workshops · Continuous Training

Quality of Training
(universe 66)

Satisfactory — 25%
41%
Unsatisfactory

have been exposed to what Lauren Resnick, director of the Learning Research and Development Center in Pittsburgh, and Daniel Resnick of Carnegie Mellon University term "high literacy."[1] Mass education, of which the United States has been so proud, really applied only to younger children and to the most basic of skills.

As young people began to stay in school longer due to lack of work opportunities or their lack of skills for more sophisticated jobs, mass education moved on to the secondary schools. However, the division between the academically privileged and "the rest" was maintained, according to Robert Hampel of the University of Delaware by "dividing the curriculum in particular ways."[2] By 1930, he writes, "roughly half of the high schools offered academic, commercial, general and vocational tracks." Hampel claims that "whether by tracks or ability groups, the school people maintained an organization that openly classified students as superior or inferior."

Justification for this practice of classifying students was established as far back as 1918 in "The Cardinal Principles of Secondary Education," enunciated by the National Education Association. Its statement proposed a vocational curriculum within the traditional high school, challenging for the first time the exclusivity of the secondary school. Even James B. Conant's seminal book, *The American High School*, published in 1958, retained the notion of different curricula, with academic excellence reserved for those considered most able to benefit from it.

Throughout the upheavals of the 1960s and 1970s, the tension persisted between the elitist and egalitarian approaches to what is taught and to whom. Periods of demand for higher academic standards alternated with times when schools were preoccupied with the social and economic factors affecting those not included in "high literacy." It was as if the two concerns could not be tended to at the same time.

The reform rhetoric of the 1980s followed this pattern, until a consensus, which emerged from diverse sources, challenged the basic premises of public education.

The Next Century Beckons

An education system fashioned specifically for the 19th and 20th century industrial revolution led by the United States is out of sync with the high-skilled workplace necessary to compete in the global economy of the new millenium. This is the theme of business and political leaders, who are pushing for radical changes in schooling. Those who decry looking upon schooling as purely utilitarian, in an economic sense, also cannot be satisfied with the status quo. Just as much evidence exists that young people are not learning how to be good citizens.

Also, American society cannot rely on the skills of those who enroll in post-secondary programs to provide the high intellectual standards characteristic of our competitors in the world market. True, about one-half of high school graduates attend postsecondary institutions. But by age 29, according to statistics from the U.S. Department of Education, only 27 percent of our young people have acquired an undergraduate degree. In other words, if future generations are to have the academic/intellectual skills to be productive, they must learn them in our nation's elementary and secondary schools.

Couple these concerns with a 40 percent increase in the number of minority students in the public schools during the 1980s and professional educators can only conclude that old premises about what and how to teach students must be reexamined.

The instructional techniques currently in use in many classrooms across the country, however, were developed when "one best system" was considered both desirable and attainable. The school's role, according to popular belief, was to teach the basics and instill good working habits adaptable to the industrial age. The idea that innovation, problem solving, cooperative work, or analytical skills were the educational right of all students was unthinkable. That these skills could be achieved by recognizing and fostering individual potential hardly was considered.

As a result in many school systems today, the traditional curriculum follows the traditional course and is still linear and limited. It does not allow much room for differences in how students learn. And too often its structure blames students when they fail to respond to the one best system.

The curriculum, Laurence Martel of Syracuse University's Center for the Study of Learning and Retention told a hearing before the New York State Board of Regents in 1988, "is not intuitive and does not convey data through spatial or visual means. It pays little attention to the whole of anything or its purpose, while elevating components, units and parts of a subject to be learned. For students who need to see the 'big picture' or to see the 'forest before the trees,' traditional education inhibits learning, contributes to stress and leads to the flight which is measured in high school attrition rates."[3]

Research on learning styles, on the other hand, Martel said, "presents a new view of learning as a cognitive catalyst among different styles, as opposed to the conventional approach which is a cognitive-deficit based model." The latter assumes

Glenbrook North High School

The "explosion" in knowledge about human health, communication and the learning process has not had as great an impact upon education as is warranted, faculty at the Glenbrook North High School in Glenbrook, Illinois, decided.

With a steering committee made up of faculty from each department with an interest in teaching learning process skills, the school spent two years studying and planning for what eventually became a Human Potential Center at the school. Its purpose is to:

- Provide a communication network among the faculty on basic process skills (drawn from research on learning styles, neurological sciences, study skills);
- Provide a vehicle for inservice training of teachers wanting knowledge about such techniques;
- Develop a coordinated outreach program in which center staff can provide presentations and assistance to teachers in the classroom;
- Create individualized and self-paced learning packets and alternative audio-visual materials for each process skill developed at the center; and
- Provide space, resources, and materials for individual and small group work, as well as for class activities.

The two-room center has a study area with materials—and simulated natural light. The other room is for relaxation. It is furnished with comfortable chairs and wireless headsets for individual or group tape listening.

The center focuses on four process skills: health, communication, thinking and study. Materials and methods take into consideration the different learning style preferences of students. Some activities are designed for small groups, others for individual learning. Audiotapes, videotapes and computer programs are all used in the center's activities. For example, under the study skill, a unit on memory consists of helping students use the pegging technique for learning an ordered list, or the substitution method for learning difficult vocabulary words.

Students come to the center often not knowing why they are doing poorly in a class, but the center staff assesses the problems by using various learning styles inventories before suggesting techniques to help. Small groups of students use the center to help with stress before a test, to improve their sports performance or to attend Success Seminars on study skills.

After a student group visited the center to learn visualization techniques, their creative writing teacher commented that the skill development made them "feel as though they were reliving an experience. They decided that this could be a valuable tool for their writing when they had to recount an experience in detail." Another teacher said she could see a difference in her students' work habits after they charted their use of time in a time management session at the center.

Students praise the center for helping them master various relaxation, visualization and memory strategies. Said one student: "I'm so glad the center is here! It's the only place I can go where nobody interrupts me!"

youngsters who have deficiencies in their information processing skills can be remediated through "augmentation," an idea first proposed by Charles Letteri, a University of Vermont psychologist.

Martel and others involved in mastery learning believe the new emphasis on cognitive learning could lead to the demise of the standard "bell curve" paradigm—the notion learners are randomly sorted across a spectrum—with an "S-curve" paradigm—in which virtually every youngster can succeed given the proper support.

We come back to the axioms for this decade, with an added sense of urgency. All children must learn, and they must achieve at a level and with the lifelong adaptabilities formerly reserved for only the few at the top. And every child has different strengths and talents which must be nurtured in order to produce the high standard of performance needed.

As Lauren Resnick points out:

"Although it is not new to include thinking, problem solving, and reasoning in **someone's** school curriculum, it is new to include it in **everyone's** curriculum. It is new to take seriously the aspiration of making thinking and problem solving a regular part of a school program for all of the population, even minorities, even non-English speakers, even the poor. It is a new challenge to develop educational programs that assume that all individuals, not just an elite, can become competent thinkers."[4]

Using what we know about learning styles is one way of ensuring that the curriculum, including high content and high expectations, engages all students.

Barriers to Learning Styles

If school administrators could agree on one obstacle to the integration of learning styles techniques, it would be teacher resistance.

"Talk is cheap," comments an Oklahoma assistant superintendent in a survey of AASA members for this publication. "Real implementation is going to take commitment on the part of the building principal and a few significant others on his staff, as well as the money to provide the training and support they will need." His district, he notes, has neither the money nor the expertise to make it happen. "Add to this a heavy dose of skepticism on the part of teachers, and the problems become much greater."

The most difficult problem, says a New Jersey superintendent, "is to get teachers to break their habit of teaching as they were taught--and learn to minimize teacher talk and maximize student participation."

A Minnesota superintendent says the same thing more bluntly. The major problem, he notes, is "a few older teachers saying and believing that it is the students and parents who have changed and it will all work out as soon as they change back to the way they were 20 or 30 years ago." Most teachers, he adds, realize that is not going to happen.

A Nebraska administrator has found teachers who have not received training in learning styles do not understand the changes made by teachers who have taken the training, "and they sometimes try to stop the different approaches, calling them wrong."

Among smaller districts, the problem of not being able to assign a staff person to coordinate and carry through on staff development and practice in learning styles prevents use of knowledge. Says a rural Oregon superintendent: "We are understaffed and can't assign formal responsibility to anyone." Further, he notes, "there are some national educators in disagreement over implementation" of learning styles research.

Others cite the lack of resources and/or time for training. A Houston administrator says his district is not integrating learning styles knowledge because of various competing demands from other programs and state requirements. And, he adds, "research on learning styles is inconclusive."

ENDNOTES

1. Resnick, Daniel P. and Resnick, Lauren B., "The Nature of Literacy: An Historical Explanation," *Harvard Educational Review*, Vol. 7, 1977, pp. 370-385.

2. Hampel, Robert, *The Last Little Citadel*, Houghton Mifflin, Boston, Mass., 1986, p. 10.

3. Martel, Laurence Dean, "Theories of Learning Styles, Neurosciences, Guided Imagery, Suggestopaedia, Multiple Intelligences and Integrative Learning," unpublished paper, Syracuse University, Syracuse, New York, 1988.

4. Resnick, Lauren, *Educating and Learning To Think*, National Academy Press, Washington, D.C., 1987, p. 7.

Chapter 2

Theories About Learning Styles

Divergent Opinions

"A decade of research indicates that students do have identifiable reading styles that predispose them to learn with ease and enjoyment through particular reading strategies, methods and materials."[1]

Marie Carbo,
Developer of reading styles inventory

"The overriding fact remains: Modality-based instruction [basing instruction on a student's strongest senses] is ineffective. Any attempt to make it appear as such by suggesting constricted instances where it might be effective is a disservice because of the potential waste of valuable instructional time. When it becomes necessary to place so many restrictions on the use of modality-based instruction to make it appear effective, such instruction becomes more fanciful than effective."[2]

Kenneth Kavale and Steven Forness,
professors of special education at University of Iowa and UCLA, respectively

Teachers intuitively know that students learn in different ways. However, until recent years this common sense about learning was often taken for granted and shadowed by other priorities for education—standardization high among them.

Sometimes it takes the imprimatur of research to catch the attention of educators. Current research about learning styles began to develop several decades ago from several different directions. These included early studies on cognitive growth, the areas of the brain related to intelligence and behavior, and the influence of school environmental and social factors on students. Added to these strains of research in recent years have been studies on the types of intelligence and factors that influence the use of intelligence and cultural conditioning for learning. But as the comments above indicate, this is a field wide open to divergent opinions.

The early research on learning styles seems simplistic compared to the knowledge now being gleaned from studies that are less empirical and more qualitatively based. However, as with initial findings about the individual factors affecting learning, conclusions are still tentative. Styles of learning represent a dynamic field, providing exciting insights that continue to evolve. Educators wishing to use knowledge about learning styles professionally, in essence, become researchers themselves, judging their new resources about student learning against their intuitions with common-sense experience.

Do Your Own Research

How can teachers determine if proponents of certain learning styles approaches have sufficient evidence for their claims?

Use standard scientific criteria, says Kathleen Jongsma of the Northside Independent School District in San Antonio, Texas, writing in the May 1990 issue of *The Reading Teacher*. She cites methods others have used to analyze learning styles research:
- publication of findings in refereed journals that employ a process of peer review;
- replication of the results by disinterested investigators in different research laboratories or classroom settings; and
- consensus within a particular research community on whether or not a critical mass of studies points toward a particular conclusion.

Using these criteria, Jongsma concludes learning styles is such a "beguiling" idea that "it can easily garner attention even in the absence of empirical evidence."

Theories that Sparked Interest

Early learning theories were deeply rooted in behaviorism, growing out of the stimulus-organism-response model. As theorists moved away from the emphasis on inputs and outputs, they had to look more carefully at the learner's characteristics—and thus the focus shifted from the physical, observable behavior (external) to cognitive/affective factors (internal).

At the beginning of this century, the notion of a fixed "intelligence quotient," or IQ, took hold in psychology. This notion is still pervasive in much of education theory today, even though court decisions have called for modifications in instruments used to determine IQ because of equity issues. As perhaps an early reaction against the idea that intelligence is immutable, the Swiss psychologist Carl Jung published *Psychological Types* in 1921, in which he argued that people "take in" information differently. He described four types: feelers, thinkers, sensors and intuitors.

Yet, says Laurence Martel of Syracuse University, learning theorists largely ignored Jung's view of acquiring information until about 15 years ago. Even today, various learning styles instruments still assume that intelligence can be measured quantitatively.

Although the term "learning style" first appeared in research literature in the 1950s and some work began to appear in the next decade by such research leaders as Paul Torrance of the University of Georgia, it did not burst upon the education scene significantly until the 1970s. More than 15 years ago Benjamin Bloom, in

Human Characteristics and School Learning, put forward a theory about the interdependent factors that account for the differences in student learning. Bloom described three key learning factors:

- what students bring to a learning task—the "cognitive entry behaviors" which they already have learned, or their learning history;
- what factors make a student want to learn—"affective entry characteristics," or motivation; and
- what learning techniques are most appropriate for the student, or the quality of instruction.

According to a summary of Bloom's research by James Keefe, director of research for the National Association of Secondary School Principals,[3] Bloom attributes most of learning effectiveness to what a student brings to school—e.g. prior knowledge and attitudes toward self and learning. Says Keefe: "When prior learning is deficient, the school's job is primarily remedial. When motivation is lacking, counseling and a measure of success are the answers. But the school can make its most significant ongoing contribution in the area of instructional quality."

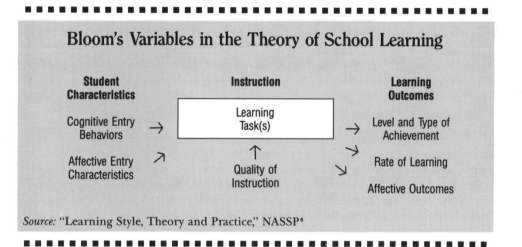

Bloom's Variables in the Theory of School Learning

Student Characteristics	Instruction	Learning Outcomes
Cognitive Entry Behaviors →	Learning Task(s)	→ Level and Type of Achievement
Affective Entry Characteristics ↗	↑ Quality of Instruction	→ Rate of Learning ↘ Affective Outcomes

Source: "Learning Style, Theory and Practice," NASSP[4]

Neither, Nor

Both heredity and environment shape intelligence, according to a carefully controlled study of adopted children conducted by researchers in France.

Children born to high-status parents who have had at least 15 years of schooling and worked as professionals had an average I.Q. 12 points higher than children born to low-status parents who have completed an average of six years of schooling and work as farmers or laborers. The researchers claim this finding suggests a strong link between heredity and intelligence.

However, the study also found children adopted by high-status families had an average I.Q. that was 15 points higher than children adopted by low-status families, regardless of the status of the birth parent. The effect of environment outweighed that of heredity in some cases.

Nurturing the Brain

Early development of the brain is indisputably linked to a child's learning ability, the National Health/Education Consortium says in a 1991 report, "Healthy Brain Development: Precursor to Learning."

Three months before birth, according to research cited in the report, a fetus "has already developed nearly the full complement of neurons—cells that serve as the functional unit of the nervous system." Once born, the environment of a child has an impact upon his/her brain. A stressful environment—malnutrition, family disorientation, drug use and exposure to lead—can negatively affect learning capacity and memory. A stimulating, safe environment can lead to maximum brain development and learning.

The report recommends that:
- Every mother and baby have early, comprehensive and preventive health care;
- All infants and children have early screening, diagnosis and treatment of learning disabilities;
- Discoveries in neuroscience be translated into the health, education and policy worlds; and
- Greater funding be provided for scientific research to promote better understanding of the complexities of the brain.

For more information, contact the National Health/Education Consortium, Institute for Educational Leadership, Suite 310, 1001 Connecticut Ave. N.W., Washington, D.C. 20036.

About the same time, David Kolb, a professor of organizational behavior and management at Case Western Reserve, developed a model based on his theory that people approach new situations primarily in two ways—through "feeling" or through "thinking." From this orientation, he divided learners into four distinct major learning styles—dynamic, imaginative, common sense and analytic learners. This model became the basis for the 4MAT system developed by Bernice McCarthy, a consultant in Barrington, Illinois.

Kolb says this about each style of learner:
- **imaginative learners** integrate experience with the self, seeking personal involvement, commitment, insight. They are interested in people and culture, approach problems reflectively, look for meaning. Because they see all sides, they sometimes have trouble making decisions.
- **analytic learners** perceive information abstractly, developing theories from integrating their observations with what is known. They want continuity, need to know what the experts think, value sequential thinking and details. They are thorough and appreciate traditional classrooms. They are engrossed in ideas and uncomfortable with subjective judgments.
- **common sense learners** integrate theory and practice. They are pragmatic, believing if something works, use it. They do not tolerate fuzzy ideas or stand on ceremony. Get to the point, is their motto. They like to tinker and experiment with things.
- **dynamic learners** learn by trial and error, integrating experience and application. They like change, flexibility, risk taking. They get enthusiastic about new things. Then can arrive at accurate conclusions in the absence of logic. They may seem pushy, but they are at ease with people.

The Four Major Learning Styles (Kolb's Circle)

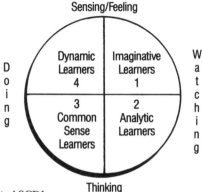

Source: *Educational Leadership*, ASCD[5]

Also in the 1970s, Anthony Gregorc, then affiliated with University of Connecticut, began working on his theories of "mindstyles," stemming from his research on cognition. He believes styles are a symptom.[6] "When viewed from a phenomenological perspective," Gregorc says, "stylistic characteristics reveal themselves to be surface indicators of two deep levels of the human mind: whole systems of thought, and peculiar qualities of the mind which an individual uses to establish links with reality."

In other words, learning style is simply one indicator of how a learner approaches reality. Such simple characteristics as a concern for detail or a strong valuing of grades "are not mere happenstance," but rather are tied to "deep psychological constructs."

According to a summary of his theories by Kathleen Butler,[7] Gregorc identifies several ways that people approach learning:

- **Concrete sequential**—the learner is structured, practical, predictable, and thorough
- **Abstract sequential**—the learner is logical, analytical, conceptual, and studious
- **Abstract random**—the learner is sensitive, sociable, imaginative, and expressive
- **Concrete random**—the learner is intuitive, original, investigative, and able to solve problems.

Some students are combinations of more than one approach.

These are examples of the theories that developed early in the study of how students approach learning differently. There are many more, some focusing entirely on cognitive research, or laboratory study, and others on applied research, especially self-perceptions of learning preferences. Some researchers honed in on the "social" characteristics of learning, providing a base for much of the cooperative learning strategies that are proving highly successful in many schools. By 1979 the field had progressed to the point that *Educational Leadership* used learning styles as a theme for an entire issue, one in which the articles focused heavily on the physiological. In October 1990 the magazine returned to the subject, tying learning styles more to brain research. From an early emphasis upon "styles," to an emphasis upon learning, to a new level of interest that concentrates on "thinking," the evolution of theories about individualizing instruction has prompted much cross-disciplinary research—and led to a rich blend of scientific and educational perspectives.

Working Definitions

Theories about learning styles may abound, but respondents to a survey by the American Association of School Administrators for this publication are nearly unanimous in what they believe learning styles means. They say it in different ways, but the message is generally the same:

"Learning styles are the dominant methods of learning favored or characterized more effective for each learner, i.e. concrete sequential, random abstract, etc."
—rural superintendent in Oregon

". . .The conditions under which you as an individual learn best."
—assistant superintendent in rural Oklahoma

"Learning styles relates to the way students acquire knowledge. For some students it is important to take small bits of information and build the big picture. Other students learn best by looking at the big picture and taking it apart piece-by-piece. The organization of instructional materials to fit the way a student learns most easily is what I consider learning styles."
—a superintendent in New York state

"Our learning style is the way we perceive the world, how we think, make judgments and form values. It is our window to the world, the unique aspect of our humaneness. Style is concerned with cognition, conceptualization, affect and behavior."
—director of instructional improvement, suburban Nebraskan district

". . .Ways children learn."
—superintendent, rural Virginia

Broadening the Discussion to Intelligence

During the 1980s, while learning styles application was becoming almost synonymous with the physiological approach, others were exploring the nature of intelligence more deeply. One of the most influential theorists has been Howard Gardner, professor of education at Harvard University and co-director of "Project Zero." His 1983 book, *Frames of Mind: The Theory of Multiple Intelligences*, suggests that human beings are capable of developing at least seven different ways of knowing the world:

- **linguistic**—sensitivity to language, meanings and the relations among words; commonly found in the novelist, poet, copywriter, scriptwriter, editor, magazine writer, reporter, public relations director, speechwriter;
- **logical**—mathematical intelligence constitutes abstract thought, precision, counting, organization, logical structure; found in the mathematician, scientist, engineer, animal tracker, police investigator, lawyer, and accountant;
- **musical**—the sensitivity to pitch, rhythm, timbre, the emotional power and complex organization of music; this is found in the performer, composer, conductor, musical audience, recording engineer, maker of musical instruments;
- **spatial**—keen observation, visual thinking, mental images, metaphor, a sense of the whole gestalt; found in architects, painters, sculptors, navigators, chess players,

naturalists, theoretical physicists, battlefield strategists;
- **bodily/kinesthetic**—control of one's body and of objects, timing, trained responses that function like reflexes; found in dancers, athletes, actors, inventors, mimists, surgeons, karate teachers and the mechanically gifted;
- **interpersonal**—sensitivity to others, ability to read the intentions and desires of others and potentially to influence them; includes consideration of others; found in politician, teacher, religious leader, counselor, shaman, salesman, manager and "people people;" and
- **intrapersonal**—self-knowledge, sensitivity to one's own values, purpose feelings, a developed sense of self; identified with the novelist, counselor, wise elder, philosopher, guru, person with deep sense of self.

All of these approaches exist to some extent in each of us. Since then, Gardner has continued to fragment intelligence. His critics wonder how far he can carry this notion of multiple intelligences.

■■■

Key Elementary School

The story of the Key Elementary School in the Indianapolis school district is one of teachers determined to bring theory they agreed with into practice—in a school they fashioned from the bottom up.

As a result, Key School began applying the ideas of Howard Gardner on multiple intelligences to the day-to-day curriculum and organization of an elementary school. In 1984 eight elementary school teachers began planning how to change what is being taught to be more engaging and successful with children; they won approval of their idea as a separate school in 1987 and selected a heterogeneous student body for grades K-6.

To carry out their belief that the several intelligences described by Gardner were equally important, the teachers who planned the school developed the faculty around the strengths they decided were needed. One-half of the staff is composed of classroom teachers, while one-half are specialists, such as full-time art, music and physical education teachers. This also meant that instructional time was spread around different specialties instead of being focused only on verbal and mathematical instruction. For example, the music teacher works with all students in the school four periods a week. As a result, all kindergarten children learn to play the violin.

"It would be nonsense to use this approach with only classroom generalists," says Patricia Bolanos, the teacher chosen by the others to be the principal of the school. "It would not have the same dynamic."

Another innovation at Key School aimed at providing opportunities for multiple talents to be fostered is the use of themes. Three themes are chosen for each year (in 1990-91 the themes were connections, patterns, and changes in time and space); all teachers use the themes and plan interdisciplinary instruction together. To broaden the children's opportunities to develop their different intelligences, the school works closely with community resources to present weekly programs related to the themes and to provide after-school activities.

Working with Gardner as a research project, the school culminates each theme's time with a videotaping of individual projects by the children. On the subject of connections, Katie, a kindergarten student, presented a project on compost which showed the interaction between garbage decay, worms and the building of a compost pile. Using the theme of patterns, third grader Heather produced and played a presentation on patterns in music, and Jeff used patterns in quilts to demonstrate the theme.

Gardner is helping the school faculty critique the use of the videotapes as tools for assessment of the students.

Key School has a waiting list and a demand from parents to continue its approach to instruction and learning in upper grades. According to Bolanos, the school district will open a secondary program built around the Key School philosophy in 1992, with the junior high school grades added first, then high school grades one year at a time.

Guggenheim School

The Guggenheim School, a K-8, all-minority school in Chicago's inner city, also adopted Gardner's theories on multiple intelligences as an overriding vision, but went about it in a different manner from the Key School. All teachers were trained in the Integrative Learning Model, developed by Laurence Martel at Syracuse University. As described by Martel, Integrative Learning combines theories and techniques drawn from a variety of disciplines, including learning styles, neurosciences, guided imagery, accelerated learning and especially multiple intelligences.

Rather than focus on deficiencies and remediation, the Guggenheim faculty used different strengths of students to help them achieve success. For example, "rap" music is used to teach material that must be learned by rote; art supports the learning of academic concepts; "living sculptures" help students use their kinesthetic talents to understand the rotation of planets or multiplication tables.

Evaluation of the Integrated Learning approach at the Guggenheim School so far has depended primarily on standardized test results, covering only the verbal and math "intelligences." However, these traditional assessments indicate the school's use of various proclivities among students paid off. In 1985, the baseline year, the school ranked at the bottom of 18 elementary schools in its area on reading and eighth in math. By 1988, it ranked fifth in both reading and math.

Integrated Learning is now being used in other schools in New York, Massachusetts, Florida, and Michigan, according to Martel.

■■

Robert Sternberg, professor of psychology and education at Yale University, is carrying the interest in styles beyond learning to "thinking styles." The ways in which students prefer to use their intelligence, he says, are as important as ability. Children—in fact, all people—need to "govern" their activities, and, in so doing, they will choose "styles of managing themselves with which they are comfortable."[8] The mind, he says, carries out its activities much as a government. The **legislative** function is concerned with creating, formulating, imagining, and planning. The **executive** function is concerned with implementing and with doing. The **judicial** function is concerned with judging, evaluating and comparing.

Mental self-government involves all three functions, but each person will have a dominant form. The hallmark of thinking styles, says Sternberg, is that they have an orientation toward one of the three functions. As he explained to a Council of Chief State School Officers' institute in 1990:

"It is important to note that any subject can be taught in a way that is congruent with any style. A literature lesson in which students put themselves in the place of an author and imagine a different ending, a history test in which they put themselves in the place of a president and imagine another way of winning a war, a science assignment for which they design an experiment—all of these are examples of **legislative** activities. Such endeavors appeal to people who like to create their own rules or structures, who like to do things in their own ways, and who enjoy dealing with problems that lack structure....

"A lecture by a teacher of literature, a short-answer or multiple-choice history test for which students must recall facts (and possibly even use them), a science assignment that focuses on the preparation of a book report—all of these are examples of **executive** activities. Pursuits of this type appeal to people who like to follow rules or guidelines, who like to be told what to do or who like to figure out which of several familiar approaches would work best, who like problems that are structured for them, and who like to recall facts....

"A literature lesson that involves comparing two literary characters, a history test that requires judging how one set of events led to another, or a science assignment that consists of evaluating an experiment—all of these are examples of **judicial** activities. Individuals who prefer such activities like to evaluate facts, procedures, and rules; like to write critiques, to give opinions, and to judge things and people...."

Sternberg admits that the theory of thinking styles "is only in its infancy" and needs much more research, even though it already seems to provide a useful way to understand performance.

In fact, if learning and thinking style research has not yet affected practice to any great extent it may well be because educators are confused by the variety of theories. And the key to any significant theory is how well it can accommodate new knowledge and new ideas and still be useful.

■■

Social Learning

"Social intelligence," one of the multiple intelligences researched by Howard Gardner at Harvard University, is being more closely studied as a clue to academic failure and behavior problems.

Children who early on become so unpopular as to be rejected by others show signs of disliking school as early as kindergarten, some studies reveal. One study of 300 elementary students found that being rejected in third grade led to a poor academic record by sixth grade. Another study of 200 students, tested first in third grade and again in 12th grade, found that the most unpopular 7-8-year-olds were twice as likely to have been arrested or to have dropped out of school.

A researcher working with Gardner isolated four major social skills in young children. Some are diplomats, able to negotiate solutions to squabbles. Others are leaders who take charge in organizing games. Others show abilities to be good friends, with sensitivity to others. And some show talents at being insightful, in understanding, for example, the reasons for the behavior of their peers. The most popular children exhibit several of these skills. The researchers also are finding that children without these skills can be helped to learn them.

The National Institute of Mental Health has awarded a three- year grant to researchers at Duke University, Vanderbilt University, the University of Washington and Pennsylvania University to study how to improve social intelligence in young children.

■■

Tentative Frameworks
■■■

The different theories and approaches to learning/thinking styles have not prevented more recent attempts to frame research and practice, however.

Most familiar to educators during the 1980s was the work of Rita Dunn, Shirley Griggs and others on learning styles that stemmed predominantly from environmental (or physiological) factors. In "Learning Styles: Quiet Revolution in American Secondary Schools,"[9] they describe learning style as "a biologically and developmentally imposed set of characteristics that make the same teaching method wonderful for some and terrible for others."

A learning style, they say, would describe how a classroom would be organized to respond to a student's needs for quiet or noise, bright or soft lighting, temperature differences, independent or group work, hearing, speaking, manipulating, or combinations of these and many other factors.

Linda H. Smith, a consultant in gifted education in Clayton, Mo., and Joseph Renzulli of University of Connecticut speak of learning styles as the counterpart of teaching styles.[10] They define learning styles in terms of the range of "instructional strategies" by which students learn: "The domain of potential teaching strategies is restricted only by the requirement that each teaching style (1) is general enough to apply to a variety of content areas; (2) is a repeatable way of teaching (i.e., can be used on different occasions); and (3) can be employed by teachers without extensive training."

They use this orientation "to eliminate the need for teachers to 'second guess' how certain psychological concepts or characteristics might relate to learning situations."

Keefe, of the National Association of Secondary School Principals, groups all of the strains of research on learning styles into three areas: cognitive styles, affective styles, and physiological styles.[11] This approach forms the basis for the definition of learning styles developed by NASSP and accepted widely:

"Learning styles are characteristic cognitive, affective, and physiological behaviors that serve as relatively stable indicators of how learners perceive, interact with, and respond to the learning environment."

Learning styles and cognitive styles sometimes are used interchangeably, says Keefe, but he notes that learning style is a broader term, covering affective and physiological as well as cognitive factors.

Cognitive styles are the preferred ways that a learner perceives, organizes, uses and retains knowledge. They are related to but different from intellectual abilities, says Keefe. Styles relate more to process, to how information is being used, while abilities "measure specific innate capacities." Cognitive styles cover such areas as sensory preferences (visual or spatial, auditory or verbal); field independence or dependence, or the importance of context in learning; impulsive versus reflective responses; and diversity versus consistency.

Affective styles refer to those aspects of personality having to do with attention, emotion and valuing, those that create a motivational process. These would cover such characteristics as persistence, curiosity, level of anxiety, locus of control, risk taking, competition versus cooperation, and social motivation.

Physiological styles "are biologically-based modes of response that are founded on sex-related differences, personal nutrition and health, and accustomed reaction to the physical environment," says Keefe. This area covers somewhat obvious factors, such as preferences for time of the day, for changing postures, or for or against certain noise levels.

Writing in 1987, Keefe noted that "not all elements of learning style are of equal importance. Some of the styles have no generally acceptable testing techniques and others are still vague enough that much more investigation is needed."

Three years later Ron Brandt of the Association for Supervision and Curriculum Development continued to express some caution.[12] "The field is young and confusing," he said.

Yet, both agreed that, as Keefe said, "learning style analysis emerges as a key element in this movement to make learning and instruction more responsive to the needs of individual students." And, added Brandt, "if we are convinced that variations (in individual strengths) are not only acceptable but desirable—we are more likely to try to adapt to them, whether we fully understand them or not."

ENDNOTES

1. Carbo, Marie, "The Evidence Supporting Reading Styles: A Response to Stahl," *Phi Delta Kappan*, December 1988, p. 323.

2. Kavale, Kenneth and Forness, Steven, "Substance Over Style: A Rejoinder to Dunn's Animadversions," *Exceptional Children*, January 1990, p. 360.

3. Keefe, James W., "Learning Style: Theory and Practice," National Association of Secondary School Principals, Reston, Va., 1987, p. 5.

4. ibid., p. 4. Reprinted with permission of the National Association of Secondary School Principals, Reston, Va.

5. Reprinted from *Educational Leadership*, October 1990, p. 32, with permission of the Association for Supervision and Curriculum Development, Alexandria, Va.

6. Gregorc, Anthony F., "Style as a Symptom: A Phenomenological Perspective," *Theory Into Practice*, Vol. 23, No. 1, p. 51.

7. Butler, Kathleen A., "Learning Styles," *Learning88*, November/December 1988, p. 31.

8. Sternberg, Robert J., "Thinking Styles: Keys to Understanding Student Performance," *Phi Delta Kappan*, January 1990, p. 367.

9. Dunn, Rita and Griggs, Shirley A., "Learning Styles: Quiet Revolution in American Secondary Schools," National Association of Secondary School Principals, Reston, Va., 1988.

10. Smith, Linda H. and Renzulli, Joseph S., "Learning Style Preferences: A Practical Approach for Classroom Teachers," *Theory Into Practice*, Vol. 23, No. 1, p. 45.

11. Keefe, pp. 7-13.

12. Brandt, Ron, "If We Only Knew Enough," *Educational Leadership*, October 1990, p. 3.

Chapter 3

Turning Theories into Research and Practice

In his seminal book, *The Structure of Scientific Revolutions*, T.S. Kuhn notes that when a new field is being investigated or undergoes a new interest, everything that is known about it has equal weight. At first no single approach or idea is strong enough to develop a paradigm. After awhile, many paradigms may develop; finally, one emerges as the accepted view.

Learning styles theorists, researchers and practitioners have not necessarily followed this traditional paradigm-building process. Because early research seemed so applicable to common-sense instruction in the classroom, many educators immediately accepted it as validating practice. As a result, learning styles research became a popular component of staff development programs before being subjected to the rigorous competition of other approaches or the intense scrutiny of prolonged investigation.

Further analysis and research on learning styles has prompted a renewed interest in the area. A number of fresh research ventures are being considered. In fact, it is apparent that learning styles will remain an open research book for some time to come because of constantly accumulating knowledge about physiological, cultural, cognitive and other processes that affect learning. On the one hand, that makes it an exciting field. On the other, it begs for caution.

Reviewing the research on learning styles, Lynn Curry, a researcher in Ottawa, Canada, found several weaknesses. Although much has been promised from the research, she says, in general "the learning style conceptualizations, and the claims made on their behalf, remain to be systematically and comparatively evaluated in practice."[1]

Nonetheless, some theories have been tested enough to yield results with enough substance to at least intrigue, if not persuade, educators of their potential importance for the classroom.

Dissecting Brain Research

In the late 1970s, educators—and many who read the current "pop" literature—were busy trying to decide if they were "left" brain or "right" brain. Analysis of one's "brain" proclivity, in many respects, prompted an interest in the identification of one's learning styles. The Yearbook of the National Society for the Study of Education in 1978 published *Education and the Brain*, which focused primarily on the implications of neurological research which portrayed the brain as having different regions for different functions.

Roger Sperry, in his groundbreaking research of the 1950s, postulated that humans basically have two brains, with each one processing information differently and both serving equally important functions. The right hemisphere uses information in a non-verbal and holistic manner; the left hemisphere, by contrast, absorbs information in a more linear, sequential and logical fashion. In recent years, researchers have added an "integrated" mode of thinking on a par with left- and right-brain dominance, positing that the two functions depend upon each other.

Another field of research on the brain, based primarily on observations of the effect of different kinds of environments on rats, contends that stimulation actually increases the weight and density of the neocortex of the brain. This has led to theories and research about the malleability of human intelligence—and the idea that stimulation can increase brain activity.

Long before these theories earned Nobel prizes, Reuven Feuerstein of Israel demonstrated the intelligence can be developed through experience (stimuli) guided by a "mediator" (parents, teachers, other adults) who provides meaning to the experience. Intelligence is not fixed, according to Feuerstein, but rather can be changed through structured cognitive development. Feuerstein's most dramatic experiments have been with young people with Down's Syndrome who gained enough skills through his Instrumental Enrichment Program to become caretakers of the elderly.

■■■

Mediated Learning in Detroit

For many special education teachers in the Detroit public schools, their students are not handicapped. Rather, they are "functioning at a lower level"—and the teachers definitely believe they can help the students learn at a higher level.

Using "mediated learning" approaches, these teachers, in a pilot program of the school district, reported early on significant changes in the social behaviors of their students. "They are more engaged with others, they seem to value themselves better, they have moved from impulsive learning to more thoughtful, active learning," says Janet Jones, coordinator of the Mediated Learning Experience Center.

The center and the teachers are integrating the teaching methods of Reuven Feuerstein, a psychologist, educator and director of the Hadassah-Wizo-Canada Research Institute in Jerusalem. Beginning his work with seriously traumatized children who survived the Holocaust, Feuerstein developed a theory that low-performing young people (and adults), including the underachieving gifted, do not suffer from deficiencies that are irremediable or inherited. Rather, they never were exposed to certain attitudes, habits and patterns of learning, he believes.

Feuerstein says that intelligence can be developed (he dismisses an immutable IQ) and that this comes about through "mediated learning." In fact, he proposes that the main goal of culture and of education should be to enable people to change, to "modify" themselves. Skills and strategies are not important, he says, because they change too frequently, but "teaching people to learn and modify themselves by learning new processes, new ways of doing things," will enable them to be lifelong learners.

The application of Feuerstein's methods to special education populations has received the most notice. He has documented, for example, the progress of Down's Syndrome youngsters from passive, rote-oriented learners to young people capable of taking care of the elderly. A few of his early special education students are now college professors.

Through extensive training in Feuerstein's methods, teachers, first of all, develop a new value system about their students—"a belief that all students can change," says Jones. The training then provides "strong, visible" instructional methods based on this belief. For example, teachers use teaching materials that are much more interactive than is customary, they ask more questions and more probing ones, and they allow students to express themselves more fully, according to Jones.

Feuerstein believes that human beings are changed in two ways—by direct exposure to stimuli and by the interaction with a mediator, e.g. parents and teachers. It is this latter influence which is unique to the human psyche, as compared to others in the animal kingdom. It is the mediator who shapes stimuli so that it makes sense to children and young people, who makes sure that the goal is not just "survival" but a life of quality, and who imposes a meaning on what is learned. The parent and teacher, says Feuerstein, should say, "I want you to see this because..." or "There is a goal in what you should do."

Unfortunately, he has observed that too many children are not receiving these "mediated learning experiences." Parents who are poor, for example, are concerned only with survival, not with quality. Their goal is food on the table, not whether it is good or looks appetizing, he notes. However, wealthier families also have stopped "mediating to their children," he says. They assume school will do it, but "a child who has come to school without the kinds of change abilities produced by mediated learning experiences will not be affected by school," he believes.

Detroit is using Feuerstein's intervention methods, primarily the "Learning Potential Assessment Device." This consists of about 400 hours of exercises, such as creating different pictures out of dots, aimed at developing habits of thinking. The exercises, however, are not endless repetitions; rather, they require "rediscovery" of the goals of learning.

The methods are being applied to younger children through a Cognitive Enrichment Network of early childhood educators in Detroit, says Jones. And a new mentoring program for special education children will provide well-trained "mediators" as case managers for the students. Her center now offers training in Feuerstein's methods, rather than having to depend upon outside consultants.

"We are learning that much of what has been the model for handicapped education is based on a belief system that some children have intelligence, and some do not," Jones explains. "Our new paradigm accepts the idea that all human beings are born with the capacity to change and be changed."

■■■

Generally, early brain research seemed to be a breakthrough in attempts to understand the different ways students approach learning. Since then, additional research has gone beyond what now has come to be considered a very simplistic view of the brain. Educators are learning—and the research is still so fluid as to not have developed a paradigm—that right- and left-brain tendencies are only part of a very complex process within the brain for dealing with stimuli. In other words, the split brain is not as important to one's capacity for learning as the sum of the parts.

For example, Nobel laureate Gerald Edelman, director of the Neurosciences Institute at Rockefeller University, contends that ascribing localized functions of the brain to strengths or weaknesses in ability to learn is too simple. Reviewing Edelman's research, Douglas Carnine, a professor in teacher education at the University of Oregon, explains that the neuroscientist believes the special centers are part of a larger procedure which he describes as categorization and recategorization.[2]

How humans carry out categorization and recategorization affects how they perceive, recognize and store information.

For educators, Edelman's views are important because of their explanation of a learner's ability to detect "sameness." It is the research on "sameness" that can help provide equal opportunity to learn in school because it explains how students make mistakes, Carnine says. The research is pretty solid on how learners make mistakes through "unintended samenesses," he says. For example, young children know that when a chair is turned in the opposite direction, it remains a chair. Similarly, when a "b" is turned, they often assume that it remains a "b" instead of becoming a "d." Making this mistake does not mean that a child has a weak visual brain function; rather, research shows that children "are more likely to confuse objects and symbols that share visual or auditory samenesses, such as 'b' and 'd.'"

Using this kind of research, Carnine says, educators can develop activities that help students learn samenesses that are appropriate and point out when they are mislearning:

> "To reduce confusion between 'b' and 'd,' for example, the curriculum designer can separate the introduction of these letters over time. When 'd' is introduced some time later, a teacher could stress the differences between 'b' and 'd,' using visual discrimination tasks before introducing auditory discrimination tasks."

Confusing Intelligence and Style ∎∎∎∎∎∎∎∎∎∎∎∎∎∎∎∎∎∎∎∎∎ ◖ ∎∎∎∎∎∎∎∎∎∎∎∎

Psychologist Robert Sternberg of Yale University has described how his theories about thinking styles have been developed through research and how they help teachers decide which students are "smart." Unless teachers take students' favored styles into account, they will confuse styles with quality of mind and unfairly label students' abilities, he cautions.

Sternberg says there are three major ways of being smart—analytic, synthetic, and practical—but only the first is typically recognized in schools.[3] Those who are analytic often are test-smart, he says. They are rewarded by the current mode of schooling, but they are not good at coming up with their own ideas.

"The result is that our schools essentially mislead students," Sternberg says. "They develop and reward them for skills that later on will be important, but much less important than they are in school. The IQ-smart children often simply disappear into the woodwork. If we look at the people who make the greatest difference to our society, they are often not the people with the highest IQs."

Test criteria tend to mislead teachers, says Sternberg. Tests are not good at measuring practical intelligence because the intelligence is embedded in context—the cultural conditioning around children. People are not all of one style of intelligence, says Sternberg, and schools need to foster all aspects of intelligence:

> "...(W)e need to recognize people who are smart in their lives are people who figure out what it is they are good at, and what it is they are not good at, and then make the most of their strengths while compensating for or remediating for their weaknesses. In other words, the most practically intelligent people are not necessarily the ones who are the highest in any of these three styles, but rather, people who figure out what it is that they are good at, and then capitalize on it: Being smart in the real world means making the most of what you have, not conforming to any preset stereotypical pattern of what others may consider smart.'"

Early Start

Research reveals a rich source of evidence on child development that suggests the interests, perspectives and patterns unique to each child begin very early and persist to adult life.

The Prospect Archive, at the Prospect School and Center in North Bennington, Vermont, includes a collection of school work from 350 students over a 20-year period. The samples were taken from the portfolios of "ordinary" students and included math papers, poems, stories, essays and various forms of art work.

According to Patricia Carini, the founder of the archive, the archive collections show that not only do patterns of learning and interests develop early, but children deal with concepts, such as time, space, motion, people and danger, very differently. Each has a characteristic style of joining his/her inner world with the outer "action" world, Carini says.

Just as the works of artists are continuous, analysis of individual student work in the archive shows that each piece created is part of one's whole way of doing things. Carini explains that an individual's work is so unmistakably that person's that it has changed her way of looking at those generalizations that refer to the child only as an instance of normative development. "It is unmistakably continuous," she says.

The archive is available for study by educators. For more information, contact Prospect Archive and Center for Education and Research, North Bennington, Vermont 05257.

Developing New Assessment Tools

Howard Gardner's theories on different intelligences led him to focus his research on one aspect—that of developing new forms of assessment that can adapt to more than the verbal and mathematical skills traditionally measured by current paper-and-pencil tests. This work is being conducted by Project Zero, a Harvard University center, and includes such projects as:

- Arts PROPEL, a collaboration of the Educational Testing Service and the Pittsburgh Public Schools to assess learning in music, imaginative writing, visual arts and other areas neglected by most standard measures.

- The use of videotapes to study student exhibitions based on a theme over time, assessing such dimensions as the conceptualizing of a project, originality, technical quality, effectiveness of presentation and collaborative skills (the "laboratory" is the Key Elementary School in Indianapolis, where the curriculum and environment are based on Gardner's ideas about multiple intelligences).

- Project Spectrum, a Boston-based research project to provide multiple stimuli in preschools and kindergartens with materials that encourage children to use different kinds of intelligences.

- Only Project Spectrum has produced sufficient data for analysis, according to Gardner and Thomas Hatch.[4] The results are "reasonably consistent" with the claims of multiple intelligence theory, they reported, with children showing relative strengths and weaknesses and with their exhibition of intelligences independent of each other.

Intervention, Inventories and Instruction

The hemispheric line of reasoning to explain learning preferences has resulted in several inventories and in research on intervention strategies. For example, the tendency to use a particular hemisphere of the brain, according to some experiments, can be influenced by changing the reinforcement used in instruction or through extensive and very specialized training. Paul Torrance, who has conducted research with gifted children, claims that a child's preferred style of learning can be changed through specific intervention techniques as quickly as in six to 10 weeks.

However, the 4MAT model developed by Bernice McCarthy is the only major one being used in instruction. She used learning style inventories developed by Torrance and Kolb to determine four learning style quadrants—innovative, dynamic, analytic and common sense. Her 4MAT model superimposes right and left hemispheric tendencies on each of the four quadrants, forming an eight-step cycle.

McCarthy's 4MAT Model

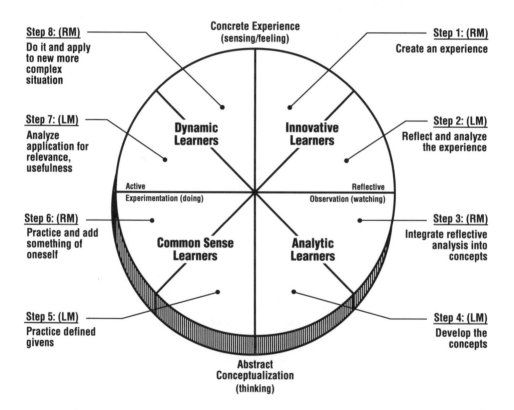

Step 8: (RM)
Do it and apply to new more complex situation

Step 7: (LM)
Analyze application for relevance, usefulness

Step 6: (RM)
Practice and add something of oneself

Step 5: (LM)
Practice defined givens

Concrete Experience
(sensing/feeling)

Dynamic Learners

Innovative Learners

Active Experimentation (doing)

Reflective Observation (watching)

Common Sense Learners

Analytic Learners

Abstract Conceptualization
(thinking)

Step 1: (RM)
Create an experience

Step 2: (LM)
Reflect and analyze the experience

Step 3: (RM)
Integrate reflective analysis into concepts

Step 4: (LM)
Develop the concepts

Source: Educational Leadership, ASCD[5]

In a presentation to a New York State Board of Regents forum on learning styles, McCarthy and Marcus Lieberman summarized research conclusions on the right-, left- and whole-brained effects upon students and their relationship to the 4MAT model.[6] They found that:

- Approximately equal percentages of boys and girls fall into each of the four learning style groups.
- During formal schooling years, students tend to favor the concrete experience dimension over the abstract dimension.
- More students were right-mode dominant than left-mode dominant.
- Each of the four learning style quadrants (see p. 24) had right-mode, left-mode, and whole-brained students.
- These brain dominance characteristics are related to sex in some as yet undetermined way.
- These brain dominance characteristics are related to age and educational experience in some complex interaction with the dimensions of concreteness and abstractness in some as yet undetermined way.
- There is a strong tendency toward left-mode in quadrants two and three and a strong tendency toward right-mode in quadrants one and four. So, the relationship between the concrete and the right mode and the abstract and the left mode is a strong one.

They describe several research studies (Fairfax County, Virginia; Kirkwood, Missouri; and North Carolina) which found positive effects by using the 4MAT model to help teachers understand students' learning styles.

■■■

Understanding Differences

Learning styles is one of five strands of the staff development program at the Millard School District in Omaha, Nebraska. The emphasis on learning styles is paying off in the classroom, reports Penny Kowal, director of instructional improvement for the district.

She describes a recent graduate class on learning styles where teachers began sharing the results of using the approach with their students. One teacher implemented the 4MAT system in a middle-level social studies class and described his decision to deviate from his usual lecture and use instead analogies and empathic understanding of differences with his eighth graders. He commented that his students "had never been involved in a discussion to the level that they were on that day." The difference, he said, was due to his decision to begin the lesson on a "feeling" level.

Recognizing that she was an "analyzer," a high school English teacher began to construct lessons that involved feelings as well as critical thinking. According to Kowal, the response among her students was "overwhelmingly favorable." She continued with the changes because so many more of her students remarked how much they enjoyed her class. Other teachers in the class reported that when they began to purposely teach to kinesthetic styles, as well as to auditory and visual, there was a noticeable increase in participation by many students.

■■■

The most detailed research on 4MAT, described in an article in *The Elementary School Journal* on a controlled group study, indicates partial success with teaching to the learning styles preferences indicated by the 4MAT approach, contrasted with traditional textbook-centered instruction.[7] The 4MAT lessons used a number of strategies—visuals, collaboration, hands-on activities and lectures, with two lessons each devoted to the four learning style preferences.

Based on a science unit with third graders from different socio-economic groups, the 4MAT instruction appeared to be superior with regard to content knowledge, comprehension, application, and analysis. Likewise, students in the 4MAT instruction had more positive attitudes toward instruction. However, according to co-authors Rhonda Wilkerson and Kinnard White of the University of North Carolina, these students did not perform any better on synthesis and evaluation than did those taught by the textbook approach.

Developing a Student Assessment

Different fields of research contributed to the development of a learning styles assessment by the National Association of Secondary School Principals. The association long has been interested in learning styles, launching a network in 1979 in cooperation with St. John's University.

Through conferences, guidebooks, and a task force, NASSP, under the guidance of its director of research, James W. Keefe, used diagnosis as the focus of its interest in learning styles. Learning style assessment, Keefe wrote in 1988, "opens the door to a more personalized approach to schooling, to student advisement and placement, to improvement of student skills, to successful instructional strategy, and to meaningful evaluation of teaching and learning."[8]

Its national task force on learning styles adopted an "umbrella" research model, first proposed by Kolb, which incorporated cognitive, affective, and physiological/environmental research areas. It borrowed from the fields of personality theory, cognitive style research, and aptitude-treatment interaction research, according to Keefe. After reviewing research on about 40 broad characteristics, the Task Force selected 24 for further research. These included:

- **Perceptual responses**—how do you get a student's attention: visually, auditorily or kinesthetically;
- **Field dependence-independence**—how a student experiences the environment, either with visual cues (field dependence) or without (field independent);
- **Successive-simultaneous processing**—preference between two forms of information processing: step-by-step (successive) or all at once (simultaneous);
- **Focusing-scanning**—ability to zero in on what's important to a problem;
- **Narrow-broad categorizing**—ability to create discrete categories to remember information;
- **Sharpening-leveling**—how a student merges new experiences, either by over-generalizing or by over-discriminating;
- **Thinking judgment-feeling judgment**—how a student reaches a conclusion, either through intellectual factors or emotional factors;
- **Achievement motivation**—striving for excellence for its own sake rather than an external reward;
- **Risk-taking-cautiousness**—a learner's willingness to take chances to reach a goal;

- **Persistence**—a learner's willingness to work beyond the minimum time, experience discomfort and face the chance of failure;
- **Time of day preferences**—a learner's response depends on the time of day, owing to the body's heat cycle;
- **Environmental elements**—a learner's preference for response to sound, light and temperature; and
- **Need for mobility**—the learner's need for a change in posture and location.

These became the basis of further review of the literature, concept papers, and a three-year pilot study that tried out learning styles profiles with thousands of students, modifying the instrument at least three times. This research, says Keefe, determined a model that includes three groups of factors:

- **Perceptual responses**—visual, emotive, and auditory
- **Cognitive skills**—spatial, analytic, sequential processing, memory, simultaneous processing, discrimination, and verbal-spatial
- **Study/instructional preferences**—mobility, posture, persistence, sound, time of day, lighting, verbal risk, manipulative, grouping and temperature.

Although the model resembles a gestalt of several elements, Keefe believes that learning style "emerges from this paradigm as an important and stable construct with a meaningful place in contemporary learning theory and practice."

■■■

Addressing Cognitive Needs, Strengths

The impact does not happen "overnight," but integrating the results of the NASSP Learning Style Profile into instruction and student support results in improved achievement, Jack Jenkins, director of the P.E. Yonge Laboratory School in Gainesville, Florida, reports.

Students in the University of Florida laboratory school are given the LSP in the sixth and ninth grades, as are students who are new enrollees in the secondary grades. The results are given to the individual student's adviser, who then makes them available to the student's teachers, upon request. In addition, all sixth graders attend a group session where the LSP's purpose and interpretation are explained; their advisers discuss the results with students individually.

Of the three areas covered by the LSP—cognitive, perceptual and instructional study preferences—the cognitive one gets the first and most prominent attention, according to Jenkins. "When we help students strengthen their cognitive skills weaknesses, they start doing better academically over time," he says. Students spend one to two hours a week in a cognitive skills center, and "we help transfer how and what students are learning in the center back to their classrooms," he explains.

A history teacher, for example, may discover that a student has weak skills in analysis. The student might be given brief passages to read in the center, then given analytical questions that are asked and answered cooperatively—in a group setting.

Using knowledge about one of his advisee's perceptual preferences, Jenkins recalls helping a student who was failing a course pull his grades up to a C. "I looked at his LSP and found out that this student preferred an auditory response," he says. The student said that he studied for tests by reading over his notes, so Jenkins advised him to read his notes aloud and to read test questions softly to himself before trying to answer them. The student showed immediate improvement.

Using the LSP, teachers also adjust students' schedules to fit the "best time of day" for particular subjects, according to Jenkins. This information is revealed in the profile's section on instructional study preferences.

A 57-year-old tradition in the university community, the Yonge Laboratory School has many long-time teachers who are not interested in using the LSP, but other teachers and Jenkins have become experts in administering and interpreting the profile. They conduct workshops for other teachers throughout the state. The school is working on a system to put the LSP individual student information in computer files for more immediate access by teachers.

An Early Instrument

One of the first inventories of learning styles to be used in classrooms is that developed by Joseph Renzulli of the University of Connecticut and Linda Smith, a consultant on gifted and talented programs in Clayton, Missouri.

Their work is based on student self-selection of learning style preferences.

A number of studies, they reported in an article in *Theory Into Practice*, found "a significant difference in student achievement and/or attitude toward subject matter when students were allowed to learn in their preferred mode of instruction."[9]

Their Learning Styles Inventory, developed in the late 1970s, consists of 65 items that give information to teachers about student attitudes toward different teaching strategies, including lecture, projects, drill and recitation, peer teaching, discussion, teaching games, independent study, simulation and programmed instruction.

Several research studies have been conducted on the inventory, particularly its use with gifted students. The general conclusion is that matching learning style preferences can have a positive effect and is a factor that can be manipulated, unlike IQ and prior achievement.

There is no definitive teaching approach, say Renzulli and Smith, but teachers who recognize the value of using a broad range of instructional strategies will more likely improve learning than teachers with a limited scope.

What's an Inventory?

A learning styles inventory is a self-report or scale that allows individual students to indicate their preferences and dislikes about specific approaches to learning.

At least a half dozen instruments available to educators are strictly inventories, or assessment tools, according to James Keefe, director of research at the National Association of Secondary School Principals. The best known is the Learning Style inventory developed by Rita Dunn of St. John's University.

Without referring to the latter or any specific inventories, Keefe suggested school leaders be cautious when considering the purchase of an inventory or learning styles program.

"A lot of people in the field are 'dog and pony show artists.' They are making a living from learning styles and you make a living not by giving general presentations on the trends in the field but by talking about your own model and the wonderful things it's going to do," he said.

An Integrative Approach

Using Anthony Gregorc's four "mindstyles," Kathleen A. Butler, head of a Connecticut educational consulting firm, The Learner's Dimension, has developed a map of learning style categories and terms. Her Style Differentiated Instruction looks like this:

Matching Your Teaching Style to Your Students' Learning Style

Styles	Characteristics	Need an instructional focus that supports	Prefer strategies such as	Styles are matched when asked to	Types of products
CONCRETE SEQUENTIAL	organized factual efficient task-oriented detailed	structure & pattern directions, details practical problems realistic situations hands-on learning	hands-on approaches workbooks data-gathering how-to projects computers	sort, label, list collect, chart make, construct class, measure prepare, build	time-line graph diorama model exhibit
ABSTRACT SEQUENTIAL	intellectual analytical theoretical critical convergent	reason & logic ideas & information theory & concepts analysis & evaluation independent study	lecture, text content mastery extensive reading reporting conceptual problems	outline, report devise, speculate infer, hypothesize summarize, verify critique	debate document theory lecture research
ABSTRACT RANDOM	imaginative emotional interpretative holistic flexible	interpretation explanation communication illustration peer-teaching	group work webbing, mapping media, music personalized examples role-playing	associate, connect relate, express share, present interpret, perform imagine, counsel	writing arts, music interview helping project journal
CONCRETE RANDOM	divergent experiential inventive independent risk-taking	open-ended activity exploration investigation experimentation options	brainstorming simulations, games problem-solving experiments finding alternatives	explore, consider reorganize forecast, process predict, create recommend	invention editorial solutions games experiments

Source: Learning88.[10]

Mindmapping Student Styles

Kathleen Butler observed each of Gregorc's four mindstyles in a classroom.[11]

Marcy, a concrete sequential learning, requires structure. She strives for accuracy and completes work on schedule. She likes hands-on activities. However, Marcy is uncomfortable in new situations, hesitates to try new things and walks away when frustrated.

Rob, an abstract sequential learner, performs best when left alone to read and think. He likes to arrive at his own conclusions, based on research and expert opinions. Yet in striving to be head of the class, Rob does not accept criticism well and gets angry when he receives a poor mark.

Liz, an abstract random learner, performs at her best when permitted to express feelings, especially in a group. She responds to questions at length. However, Liz has trouble working independently and finds it difficult to focus on detailed instructions.

David, a concrete random learner, succeeds best when he can experiment and generates a wellspring of creative ideas. Yet David has little patience for fine details and has trouble offering reasons for the conclusions he has reached.

Butler contends teachers find the mindstyles guide very helpful in putting a framework around their own intuition about good teaching. Children and teachers combine aspects of all four styles, she says, but most work naturally with one or two of them. Some children show a dominant style early; others may take a long time to reveal preferences.

The 'Environmental' Approach

A group of researchers affiliated primarily with the Center for the Study of Learning and Teaching Styles at St. John's University in Jamaica, New York, early on promoted the importance of responding to students' individual learning styles in order to improve achievement and behavior. The researchers include Rita Dunn, director of the center; Kenneth Dunn, professor at Queens College, Flushing, New York; Shirley Griggs; Marie Carbo, who has specialized in students' reading styles; and other faculty and doctoral students at St. John's University.

The Dunns published *Teaching Students Through Their Individual Learning Styles* in 1978. With Carbo, they wrote *Teaching Students to Read Through Their Individual Learning Styles* in 1986. Their research also has been published extensively by NASSP and the Association for Supervision and Curriculum Development.

Citing results from almost 20 research studies, Rita Dunn and others define learning style as "a biologically and developmentally imposed set of personal characteristics that make the same teaching method effective for some and ineffective for others."[12] Their citations lean heavily on physiological, sociological and environmental factors related to learning styles. For example, research by Dunn contends that four elements affect from 10 percent to 40 percent of students (depending on age, gender, hemisphericity and achievement)—quiet versus sound, bright or soft lighting, warm or cool temperature, and formal versus informal seating designs.

Griggs and Dunn and V.J. Tappenden found that vocational students tend to not be "morning people." Generally, their studies on time preferences found most students are not alert in the mornings, the researchers suggest.[13]

They also note that more than 70 percent of school-age children are affected by perceptual preferences. Even high school teachers, they say, find that using manipulatives, visuals and other resources that can match individual preferences increases student achievement and interest.

Conflicting Claims

The validity and conclusions of some research cited by Dunn and others has come into question, however. In an exchange with Dunn in *Exceptional Children*,[14] Kenneth Kavale of University of Iowa and Steven Forness of UCLA contend that research on types of preferences, leading to determination of individual learning styles, "for the most part...has not yielded the promised results."

Analyzing 39 research studies of learning styles, Kavale and Forness concluded that the evidence "indicates essentially no effect for modality (based on types of preferences) teaching....Any attempt to make it appear as such (effective) by suggesting constricted instances where it might be effective is a disservice because of the potential waste of valuable instructional time."

Similarly, Carbo's research on the relationship of learning styles to reading achievement was criticized by Steven Stahl of Western Illinois University for flawed methodology in the December 1988 *Phi Delta Kappan*.[15] Carbo, on the other hand, accuses Stahl of bias toward phonics instruction in the same issue and cites numerous research studies using her Reading Style Inventory which found that matching students' reading styles "results in significant gains in reading comprehension, better attitudes toward reading, and more reading for pleasure, particularly for at-risk students."

Putting Research into Practice

Reviewing the controversy over research results, education journalist John O'Neil concludes that "allegations and countercharges of shoddy scholarship and vested interests have clouded the issue and made it all the more difficult for practitioners to decide what's worth pursuing."[16]

How are educators actually using learning styles? This question was asked of Pat Guild, director of graduate education programs at Antioch University in Seattle and the author of *Marching to Different Drummers*, and her explanation categorizes much of the research threads:

"Broadly there are three different approaches. There's a focus on the individual: know thyself. And know the other person you're interacting with. It's very important for an educator when working with another person to understand in depth what both are like. Personal awareness is an aspect of all learning style treatments, but some advocates emphasize it more than others—Tony Gregorc, for example, and to a certain extent the Myers-Briggs people [developers of an instrument to assess personality types].

"Another aspect of learning styles is application to curriculum design and to an instructional process. Knowing that people learn in different ways, you use a comprehensive model that provides for the major differences. That's the approach taken by Bernice McCarthy, Kathy Butler, and several others.

"The third approach is diagnostic/prescriptive. You identify key elements of the individual's learning style, and as much as possible, match your instruction to those individual differences. That's the method espoused by Rita and Ken Dunn and by Marie Carbo."[17]

ENDNOTES

1. Curry, Lynn, "A Critique of the Research on Learning Styles," *Educational Leadership*, October 1990, p. 54.

2. Carnine, Douglas, "New Research on the Brain: Implications for Instruction," *Phi Delta Kappan*, January 1990, pp. 372-377.

3. Sternberg, Robert J., "Styles of the Mind," paper prepared for the 1990 Summer Institute of the Council of Chief State School Officers.

4. Gardner, Howard and Hatch, Thomas, "Multiple Intelligences Go To School," *Educational Researcher*, November 1989, pp. 4-9.

5. Reprinted from *Educational Leadership*, October 1990, p. 33, with permission by the Association for Supervision and Curriculum Development, Alexandria, Va.

6. McCarthy, Bernice and Lieberman, Marcus, "Learning Styles Dialogue," EXCEL Inc., Barrington, Ill., 1988.

7. Wilkerson, Rhonda and White, Kinnard, "Effects of the 4MAT System of Instruction on Students' Achievement, Retention, and Attitudes," *The Elementary School Journal*, March 1988, pp. 357-368.

8. Keefe, James W., *Profiling and Utilizing Learning Style*, National Association of Secondary School Principals, Reston, Va., 1988.

9. Smith, Linda and Renzulli, Joseph, "Learning Style Preferences: A Practical Approach for Teachers," *Theory Into Practice*, Volume 23, No. 1, pp. 44-50.

10. Reprinted from *Learning88*, November/December 1988, p. 30-34, with permission of the Springhouse Corporation, Springhouse, Pa.

11. Butler, Kathleen A., "Learning Styles," *Learning88*, November/December 1988, pp. 30-34.

12. Dunn, Rita, Beaudry, Jeffrey and Klavas, Angela, "Survey of Research on Learning Styles," *Educational Leadership*, March 1989, pp. 50-58.

13. ibid., p. 55.

14. Kavale, Kenneth and Forness, Steven, "Substance Over Style: Assessing the Efficacy of Modality Testing and Teaching," *Exceptional Children*, November 1987, pp. 228-239; and "Substance Over Style: A Rejoinder to Dunn's Animadversions," *Exceptional Children*, January 1988, pp. 357-361.

15. Stahl, Steven A., "Is There Evidence to Support Matching Reading Styles and Initial Reading Methods?" *Phi Delta Kappan*, December 1988, pp. 317-322.

16. O'Neil, John, "Findings of Styles Research Murky at Best," *Educational Leadership*, October 1990, p. 7.

17. Brandt, Ron, "On Learning Styles: A Conversation with Pat Guild," *Educational Leadership*, October 1990, p. 10.

Chapter 4

Learning Style Strategies and Tools

Despite the infancy and volatility of learning styles research, many school districts and schools are using learning styles tools to help teachers understand the importance of differences and to broaden their teaching strategies.

The movement is linked to research in other areas, such as the benefits of cooperative learning or intervention strategies to compensate for the effects of poverty.

There are as many as 20 popular inventories now in use, according to Laurence Martel of Syracuse University.[1] Based on the researchers or their models, he divides them into several major groups:

- Matching learners to their styles (Dunn)
- Cycling learners through environments which employ each style in instruction (McCarthy)
- Matching supervision strategies and instruction to the brain hemisphere and limbic system dominance profile (Herrman)
- Managing parental behavior, teaching style and children's behavior in terms of differences in dominance patterns (Reckinger)
- Exploring cultural and bi-cultural factors on learning (Hill and Ramirez)

No review of the tools available can be completely inclusive, but there are inventories which appear to be more prominently used than others.

Learning Style Inventory

Developed by Rita Dunn, Kenneth Dunn and Gary Price, the Learning Style Inventory is used in both elementary and secondary schools and leans heavily on affective and physiological effects. The inventory groups influences upon learning into four general categories—environmental, emotional, sociological, and physical. A self-reported questionnaire, with more than 100 items, asks students to identify their learning preferences. The instrument is computer-scored. Elements include:

- **Environmental**—sound, light, temperature, design
- **Emotional/psychological**—motivation, persistence, responsibility, structure
- **Sociological**—self-oriented, colleague-oriented, authority-oriented, pair-oriented, team-oriented, varied
- **Physical**—perceptual, intake, time, mobility.

Originally developed for grades 3-12, there now are parallel questionnaires for grades 1-2 and for adults.

Reading Styles Inventory
■■

A contributor to the Dunn/Dunn/Price inventory, Marie Carbo has applied the same research base to focus on reading styles. She groups beginning readers under two general categories—global and analytic—and has developed a checklist that helps determine a young student's preferences. The Carbo approach also recommends appropriate teaching strategies and materials.

■■■

Global/Analytic Reading Styles Checklist

Scoring:	
Strongly Analytic	14–18
Moderately Analytic	9–13
Fairly Analytic	4–8
Slightly Analytic	0–3

Analytic Students Often:

____ 1. Process information sequentially and logically.
____ 2. Solve problems systematically.
____ 3. Concentrate and learn when information is presented in small, logical steps.
____ 4. Enjoy doing puzzles (e.g., crossword, jigsaw).
____ 5. Like to follow step-by-step directions.
____ 6. Can understand a rule without examples.
____ 7. Enjoy learning facts such as dates and names.
____ 8. Enjoy learning rules and using them.
____ 9. Enjoy learning phonics.
____ 10. Understand and apply phonic rules.
____ 11. Recall letter names and sounds easily.
____ 12. Can decode words out of context.
____ 13. Recall low-interest words (e.g., "what," "fan") almost as easily as high-interest words (e.g., "elephant," "monster").
____ 14. Are critical and analytic when reading.
____ 15. Can identify the details in a story.
____ 16. Recall many facts after listening to and/or reading a story.
____ 17. Easily list story events in logical, sequential order.
____ 18. Like to do reading skill exercises.

Global Students Often:

____ 1. Concentrate and learn when information is presented as a gestalt or whole.
____ 2. Respond to emotional appeals.
____ 3. Tend to like fantasy and humor.
____ 4. Get "wrapped up" in a story and do not concentrate on the facts.
____ 5. Process information subjectively and in patterns.
____ 6. Need to know the essence of a story before reading/hearing it.
____ 7. Need examples of a rule to understand the rule itself.
____ 8. Understand "concrete" examples better than those that are "abstract."
____ 9. Easily can identify the main ideas in a story.
____ 10. Are unconcerned about dates, names, or specifics.
____ 11. Recall information easily when it is presented in the form of an anecdote.
____ 12. Will concentrate and pay attention better if the goal of the lesson is clearly stated at the beginning.
____ 13. Need to learn with high-interest, meaningful materials.
____ 14. Do not enjoy doing isolated skill exercises.
____ 15. Are able to learn a reading skill if the lesson is DRAWN from a story already read.
____ 16. Understand better if a story is enhanced by visuals (drawings, cartoons, photographs).
____ 17. Recall high-interest words ("elephant," "circus," "dinosaur") much more easily than low-interest words (e.g., "met," "bet").
____ 18. Use story context to figure out unknown words.

Source: Exceptional Children, Council for Exceptional Children[2]

■■

Reading Styles Profile

The National Reading Styles Institute is embarking on a national research project involving 3,000 students in 10 districts, based upon positive results from pilot programs using the reading styles inventory.

In Pine Bluff, Arkansas, for example, one first grade teacher reported that all of her Chapter 1 students were reading at grade level after the teacher incorporated the Recorded Book Method into instruction. This is a strategy developed by Marie Carbo, using oral renditions of a basal textbook.

According to Willis Alderson, superintendent at Pine Bluff, this 17-year veteran teacher had never obtained such success in reading with students before. Both she and the Chapter 1 instructional assistant had received training in using the recorded book method.

Another anecdotal example from Pine Bluff is that of a remedial reading class student experimenting with the use of colored overlays, also a technique used in reading styles teaching. At the end of class, the student, ordinarily shy, asked the teacher if she could take the red overlay with her to her other classes. This was the first time, she explained, that "the words didn't run off the page."

With a Rockefeller Foundation grant, the district's reading coordinator, Rebecca Thomasson, studied the effect of the reading styles inventory and strategies upon young readers. In an eight-month experiment with Chapter 1 students, their reading comprehension gains were significantly higher than the previous year. A much shorter experiment yielded no statistically significant gains in achievement.

However, Thomasson reported improved teaching strategies. These included a 38 percent increase in peer tutoring, 20 percent fewer discipline problems, 44 percent increase in smiles by teachers and students, 23 percent increase in cooperative learning, 52 percent increase in the use of overhead projectors, and a 17 percent increase in communication with parents.

About 70 percent of the teachers are now using their knowledge of reading styles most of the time, reports Alderson.

NASSP Learning Style Profile
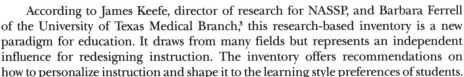

The National Association of Secondary School Principals has worked for more than a decade in the learning styles field. NASSP initially conducted research to determine its importance and then developed an instrument through long-term studies conducted at research university centers (University of Vermont, Ohio State University and St. John's University).

NASSP research also divides learning style preferences into four general categories—cognitive styles, perceptual responses, student preferences and instructional preferences. The Learning Style Profile includes 23 factors under these categories:

- Analytic skill
- Spatial skill
- Discrimination skill
- Categorizing skill
- Sequential processing skill
- Memory skill
- Perceptual response; visual
- Perceptual response; auditory
- Perceptual response; emotive
- Persistence orientation
- Verbal risk orientation
- Verbal-spatial preference
- Manipulative preference
- Study time preference: early morning
- Study time preference: late morning
- Study time preference: afternoon
- Study time preference: evening
- Grouping preference
- Posture preference
- Mobility preference
- Sound preference
- Lighting preference
- Temperature preference

According to James Keefe, director of research for NASSP, and Barbara Ferrell of the University of Texas Medical Branch,[3] this research-based inventory is a new paradigm for education. It draws from many fields but represents an independent influence for redesigning instruction. The inventory offers recommendations on how to personalize instruction and shape it to the learning style preferences of students.

4MAT

The premises of the 4MAT system are that people have different learning styles based on hemispheric preferences (following Kolb's model) and that designing instruction to respond to these modes can improve teaching and learning. The 4MAT program focuses on designing instruction to follow a full circle of learning style preferences. In each quadrant, specific instructional strategies cater to the styles represented in the quadrant. Putting the strategies together builds a complete cycle of opportunities for all students to have access to learning; then the cycle is repeated, building on the skills of each successive cycle.

The 4MAT Process as System

PRINCIPAL **The Refocuser** **4**	• Rearticulating meaning • Setting up collaboration possibilities • Helping people learn from failure • Championing good tries • Coordinating evaluation • Enlarging diffusion networks • Labeling the successes which will become harbingers of strategic new directions	• The WHY of the school • The spirit communicated with enthusiasm, passion, and hope • Accomplished by honoring teacher diversity as strength, by aligning and bonding people • The courage to create a mission statement and to articulate its meaning	**PRINCIPAL** **The Meaning** **Articulator** **1**
TEACHER **The Facilitator of** **Creative Options**	• Overseeing student self-discovery • Arranging student sharing • Encouraging diverse use of learning • Elaborating • Critiquing • Honoring student originality	• Helping to forge connections between the content and the students' lives • Honoring student diversity as an aid to learning • Honoring teacher diversity as resources to each other	**TEACHER** **The Meaning** **Connector**
STUDENT **The Innovator** **QUADRANT FOUR: "IF?"** • Maximizing uniqueness • Discovering together as a school community • Encouraging distinct competence • "If?" demands synergy	• Applying learning in new ways	• Connecting personal life and the content **QUADRANT ONE: "WHY?"** • Vision is critical • We have the most compelling need for ideas	**STUDENT** **The Meaning** **Maker**
QUANDRANT THREE: "HOW DOES THIS WORK?" • Ideas do not become mine because I read them. I must act on them. • Actions inform thought • Ability must be exercised		**QUADRANT TWO: "WHAT?"** • The content must be significant and presented with whole-brained techniques • Learning must be understood in its multiple forms	
STUDENT **The User of** **Content and Skills**	• Practicing and personalizing	• Understanding at the conceptual level	**STUDENT** **The** **Comprehender**
TEACHER **The Sponsor and** **Practice Coach** **3**	• Guiding and facilitating basic skill development • Leading students to the identification and articulation of the material learned • Leading students to the use and integration of the material learned	• Managing and delivering knowledge units with conceptualized themes patterned into meaningful connections • Relating the parts back to the whole	**TEACHER** **The** **Instructional** **Leader** **2**
PRINCIPAL **The Facilitator** **of Resources**	• Honoring multiple methods of instruction • Arranging time, money, and materials • Setting up environments open to testing and experimenting • Generating opportunities • Guiding the diffusion process	• Aligning curriculum with the mission statement • Overseer of the entire curriculum conceptualization, systemization, and connection • Consistently holding the idea of "process" and "product" as parallel goals • Planner of systematized staff development	**PRINCIPAL** **The** **Instructional** **Coordinator**

Source: Educational Leadership, ASCD[4]

The 4MAT approach is more of an instructional strategy or lesson-planning exercise than an inventory. It requires a systematic view, in which instruction is tied to curriculum, evaluation, and the structure and organization of time for both teachers and students, says McCarthy.[5]

Generally Speaking
■■■

Reviewing more than 100 learning style instruments, Lynn Curry selected eight as being particularly appropriate for secondary schools. Her research discussion, published by the National Center on Effective Secondary Schools at the University of Wisconsin,[6] presents a taxonomy and maps their emphases:

■■■

Learning Style Taxonomy and Contributions of Learning Style to Learning Outcomes

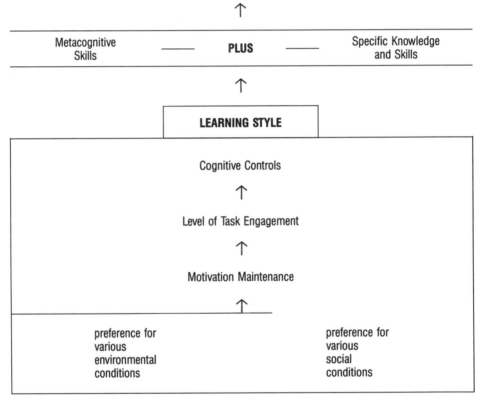

Source: National Center on Effective Secondary Schools[7]

■■■

Curry cautions, however, that the research evidence to support important claims about learning styles and the validity of diagnostic instruments "have not been systematically evaluated in practice."

"Adaptive education," or flexibility, may be the best course for educators interested in applying learning style concepts, Curry says, explaining:

"Students are ill-suited to a curriculum when either the student has not mastered the necessary content background or supporting knowledge and skills, or has not developed the information processing approach (cognitive control) required by the particular curriculum. Depending on the situation and the student, a teacher could choose to concentrate on direct training of the missing content knowledge and skills and perhaps direct training of the necessary information processing approach (cognitive control). Alternatively, the teacher could choose to proceed with content instruction in an entirely new manner which does not require prior mastery of the 'missing' content knowledge, skills and information processing. By making either of these choices the teacher could conceivably preserve student motivation and self-esteem while the missing information or approach is learned. To make either adaptive choice requires information about the student, some of which may be provided through various of the learning style concepts and measurements systems."

Whether learning styles inventories and models are *the* tools to individualizing learning or *a potentially useful* tool remains an open question at this point. What is certain, however, is the benefit described by Asa Hilliard of Georgia State University: "Perhaps the most significant thing about the discussion of styles and learning is that it provides the opportunity to raise issues pertaining to pedagogy that would not be raised otherwise."[8]

■■■

Does Culture Create a Learning Style?

The effect of culture and ethnicity upon learning is only beginning to provide useful signals to the classroom teacher.

The key questions researchers are addressing are these: what are the individual cognitive styles produced by a student's African-American, Native American or Hispanic cultural heritage and how should educators use them to enhance student learning?

Laurence Martel, director of the Center for the Study of Learning and Retention at Syracuse University, says the field of learning styles "among specific cultures holds great promise of moving toward a more accommodating, responsible and energetic vision of learning as a truly multi-cultural, multi-lingual and multi-dimensional opportunity."

Asa Hilliard, a professor of urban education at Georgia State University, has studied variations of learning styles among cultural groups. He has identified three problem areas:

- errors in estimating a student's intellectual potential, leading to misplacement and mistreatment;
- errors in estimating a student's learned achievement in subjects such as reading; and
- errors in estimating a student's language ability.

When a teacher misunderstands culture, a major conflict may arise in the classroom. Jacqueline Irvine of Emory University has cited several issues that lead to cultural conflicts:

- personal presentation styles of some students, such as their style of walking or dress;
- non-verbal and verbal communication styles, such as teasing rituals or "stylized sulking;"
- language, including different assumptions about what is spoken and left unspoken; and
- cognition, such as a predisposition toward learning through freedom of movement, inductive reasoning and a focus on people.

To improve the achievement of culturally different students, Barbara Robinson Shade, dean of the School of Education at University of Wisconsin-Parkside, says educators need to think seriously about changes in the following areas:

- social control of students, which may differ markedly from what is exercised by parents;
- classroom climate, which should consider open spaces, open discovery and use of inductive thinking approaches;
- expectations for success, communicated regularly to all students; and
- development of strategies to perform various content tasks.

Shade and Hilliard agree on the primary barrier to integrating cultural behavior strengths into the curriculum and instruction: the lack of will.

■■

ENDNOTES

1. Martel, Laurence Dean, "Theories of Learning Styles, Neuroscience, Guided Imagery, Suggestopaedia, Multiple Intelligences and Integrative Learning," paper delivered to New York State Board of Regents, March 1988.

2. Reprinted from *Exceptional Children*, summer 1988, p. 56, with permission of the Council for Exceptional Children, Reston, Va. Copyright (c) 1988.

3. Keefe, James and Ferrell, Barbara, "Developing a Defensible Learning Style Paradigm," *Educational Leadership*, October 1990, pp. 57-61.

4. Reprinted from *Educational Leadership*, October 1990, p. 35, with permission of the Association for Supervision and Curriculum Development, Alexandria, Va. Copyright (c) 1990.

5. McCarthy, Bernice, "Using the 4MAT System to Bring Learning Styles to Schools," *Educational Leadership*, October 1990, pp. 31-37.

6. Curry, Lynn, "Learning Styles in Secondary Schools: A Review of Instruments and Implications for Their Use," National Center on Effective Secondary Schools, University of Wisconsin-Madison, 1990.

7. Reprinted from "Learning Styles in Secondary Schools: A Review of Instruments and Implications for Their Use," with permission from the National Center on Effective Secondary Schools, University of Wisconsin-Madison.

8. Hilliard, Asa, "Behavioral Style, Culture, and Teaching and Learning," paper presented to the New York State Board of Regents, March 1988.

Chapter 5

A Practical Guide for Educators

How does one navigate the sometimes murky and choppy waters of learning styles? For many practitioners, charting a smooth and steady course has not been easy. As school reform winds change and educational research currents shift, educators quickly discover that there are many ports on the horizon.

Both veteran and aspiring school leaders know there is much to be gained from the knowledge and experiences of those who have embarked on similar ventures. Many have found that the path of implementation is often marked with any number of valid questions and demanding challenges.

To help teachers and administrators determine their bearings and map a course that seems right for their schools or classrooms, we have turned to the experts—teachers, administrators, staff developers, and a research director. Here are their responses to some of the questions you might ask about learning styles.

How do most teachers find out about learning styles?

Bob Bates, a middle school math teacher at the Heath School in Chestnut Hill, Massachusetts, first encountered learning styles about four years ago at a teacher workshop. Since then, Bates has pursued extensive training in the 4MAT model and has served as a consultant to teachers in other content areas.

Terry Foriska, a middle school assistant principal in Pittsburgh, Pennsylvania, says his concern about children and what they need to succeed in school led him to a National Association of Secondary School Principals seminar on cognitive styles.

Other teachers and principals have come upon the learning styles approach through their reading in professional journals, conversations with colleagues, or university courses for recertification and advanced degrees. A number of undergraduate and graduate programs offer specific courses in learning styles theory, research and practice.

For many practitioners, though, their first exposure is just enough to pique their interest because they can see how it applies to themselves as well as to their students and fellow staff. Bobby Prewitt, a former elementary teacher and now a consultant/trainer with the Learner's Dimension, says often a teacher's initial encounter is an "aha" experience. Coming from classrooms of increasing diversity, they see how the approach can help them accommodate the different needs of students. It is this personal discovery and professional awareness that appeals to people and is also essential for implementation and long-term application.

Yet, for some teachers, this first encounter is less than happenstance and enlightening. A school principal, for example, may "turn on" to the learning styles approach or a particular model and try to sell it to teachers by bringing in a consultant for staff development. Unless the teachers see its relevance and buy into it, explains

Helene Hodges, research director for the Association for Supervision and Curriculum Development, this type of top-down initiative will fall flat.

A former teacher, Hodges advises administrators to consider carefully how to introduce and incorporate the learning styles approach into the everyday life of the school, its staff, students, and community.

What type of school climate will foster style-based learning? What can the principal do to help staff incorporate learning styles?

One thing the experts agree on is that incorporating a style-based approach can prompt systemic change. It impacts not only classroom instruction, but also school organization, management and communication. Incorporating style-based learning necessitates continual feedback, coaching and modeling among staff, says Hodges. And this feedback must be offered in a non-threatening way.

Hodges recommends beginning with a needs analysis. Staff should look at the nature of challenges, problems and issues that exist at both school-wide and classroom levels and whether a learning styles approach seems appropriate.

In 1989, in response to a staff development needs analysis, a team of teachers and administrators from the Aberdeen, South Dakota, Public Schools attended an institute at the Center for the Study of Learning and Teaching Styles in New York City. There they worked with Rita Dunn, Ken Dunn and staff at St. John's University. When they returned, the team formed a district-wide Learning Styles Steering Committee. Building-level task forces followed, and though each teacher was required to attend a three-day learning styles workshop, classroom implementation of the approach was voluntary.

Duane Alms, principal at C.C. Lee Elementary School in Aberdeen, says staff at his school "have had tremendous success with learning styles." The school has been selected as one of eight nationwide to be featured in a forthcoming learning styles handbook compiled by the Dunns for the National Association of Elementary School Principals.

According to Alms, since implementing the Dunn and Dunn model and using the Learning Styles Inventory, school staff have witnessed gains in student performance on standardized tests, and this has happened across grade levels and content areas. Noting the student population at C.C. Lee is very stable, Alms says he can think of no other reasons why student scores would go up, other than the teachers' efforts to use the learning styles assessment to better accommodate student learning needs. So far, about 85 percent of the faculty have indicated they are using learning styles in varying degrees. Alms says there is strong administrative support for its implementation and that it has become part of the building goals and agenda.

In some other schools, the principal has tapped a small cadre of teachers to train and then implement style-based instruction, hoping others will start asking questions and become interested. This is the strategy Foriska, in Pittsburgh, took. He began with a group of about three teachers who were interested in professional and personal improvement and who were very dedicated to their students. In three years, he has seen support swell and remarkable changes in the attitude of teachers who had 18-19 years of experience and had seemed "pretty much set in their ways."

For the approach to catch on and gain wide acceptance, a school climate that emphasizes awareness and appreciation of differences is critical. Bob Erickson, a staff development specialist and former secondary teacher in St. Louis Park, Minnesota, contends that climate begins with the principal who has to take a close look at whom he or she hires and how he or she manages people. The principal also plays a vital role in helping teachers understanding their own style preferences and those of their colleagues.

■■■

NEA On Mastery Learning

Since the mid-1980s, the National Education Association has been looking at issues related to school renewal and restructuring. Not surprisingly, an area that has garnered a lot of attention has been instructional strategies and, particularly, learning styles. Over the years, says Robert McClure, of NEA's Mastery Learning Program, a network of teachers, site-based administrators and staff, parents, and other professional educators has evolved to discuss issues, share information, and participate in field research.

According to McClure, two positive outcomes have evolved from the discussions, the exchange of information, and field studies on learning styles.

First, teachers have begun to examine more closely their own teaching. This increased awareness has fostered an individualized, client-centered approach to teaching and offers strategies for altering services within classrooms and school settings.

Second, McClure explains, it has prompted a number of teachers who "are on the cutting edge" to begin questioning the use of labels and the appropriateness of categories in working with students. Many of these teachers are asking whether we are not really talking about differences in learning styles, rather than differences in learning abilities and disabilities.

Overall, a focus on learning styles offers promise for change in the way teachers work with our students, and, thus, the schools' clients, McClure says. As a result, teachers report witnessing "huge breakthroughs with children, we, in the past, had not held out much hope for," he adds.

NEA publications on learning styles include "Learning and Thinking Styles: Classroom Interaction" and "Learning Styles: What Research Says to the Teacher." Both are available from the NEA Professional Library, 1201 16th Street, N.W., Washington, D.C. 20036 (202-822-7250).

■■■

With so many models of learning styles, how does a teacher know where to begin and which one to use?

Unless there is a comprehensive professional development program that includes learning styles, most principals and teachers will have to assume responsibility for seeking those resources which will provide an overview of the theoretical foundations, research, and different models. Journals and special publications by professional organizations, such as ASCD, NASSP, NAESP and AASA, offer a rich source of information and references.

As usual, common sense prevails. Hodges advises practitioners to base their decisions on sound theories regarding child development, cognition, hemisphericity and learning. She also suggests teachers look at which instruments have undergone the most rigorous research and to look for both distinctions and links among models.

Prewitt also advocates a common sense approach to selection. She says teachers need to base their decisions on what they know about their students. Does the model deal with the whole child and his or her entire range of needs and abilities? Does it encourage creative and critical thinking? Does it put information in the hands of the teacher so she or he is the decision-maker? Prewitt says she decided to use the Learning Dimensions model, which is based on Gregorc's mindstyles, because it offered a lot of flexibility and emphasized problem-solving.

One of the challenges in getting started is getting beyond learning styles jargon. The different theories, research, models and instruments have their own terminology. Theories form the foundation for models and research. Some models are more research-based than others; most models provide a framework for specific instructional methods and strategies. Instruments to determine one's style preference may be in the form of an observational checklist used by the teacher or a pencil-and-paper inventory completed by the learner. Some models include diagnostic instruments, and some do not.

Denise Verley Matthews, a physical disabilities teacher in Falls Church, Virginia, favors Maria Carbo's Reading Styles Inventory, though she is familiar with and has used other instruments and models. While she has found the 4MAT model is congruent with the integrated language arts approach, Matthews tries to vary instruction to appeal to different sensory modes, global and analytical preferences, and to actively engage students in making choices.

In summary, some teachers prefer one model over others. Others, like Matthews, incorporate a variety of strategies stemming from several different models. According to Erickson, "teachers get to the point where they know what they want"—based on their needs and the needs of their students.

■■

AFT On Learning Style

Teacher interest in learning styles is difficult to gauge, according to Debbie Walsh, associate director of educational issues at the American Federation of Teachers. Often inquiry regarding learning styles surfaces as part of larger questions, such as how to better meet individual student needs, how to make learning more active, or how to restructure classrooms and schools.

Though AFT has consulted with a number of nationally recognized experts in examining learning style theory, research, and application, there are still a lot of unanswered questions, particularly about the validity of the research. What is critical, at this point, according to Walsh, is first trying to figure out what the critical questions are, with regard to learning styles, and then determining what to do with the answers.

■■

What are some specific ways learning styles might be implemented in the classroom?

The application of learning styles in the classroom will depend, of course, upon the model or models the teacher prefers and finds most helpful in working with students. At C.C. Lee Elementary School in Aberdeen, South Dakota, for example, a sixth grade teacher discovered from the Dunn and Dunn Learning Styles Inventory that one of her students had distinct preferences for specific learning design elements. The child learned best in a private setting with low light, a hard work surface, and quiet.

To accommodate the student's needs during independent practice and when encountering new and difficult work, the teacher provided a private study carrel in a corner of the room away from the direct glare of overhead fluorescent lighting and situated so that the student's back was toward the rest of the class. In addition, the student also was given headsets to cut down on noise and interruptions. Within three months, the teacher reported that the child had demonstrated improved performance on standardized tests.

At Centennial Elementary in Littleton, Colorado, Principal Colin Powell says 4MAT has become a standard model for planning teacher in-service. When staff became interested in a futures-based model of education developed through a district grant, the lead teachers who had been involved in the innovative project decided to use the 4MAT cycle to appeal to the different learning styles of their colleagues. Since then, Powell says teachers have made a conscious effort among themselves to model the 4MAT approach in their staff presentations.

Mike Greenwood, an elementary teacher in Windsor, Connecticut, has discovered training in critical thinking dovetails nicely with 4MAT. For a social studies unit on western European expansion, Greenwood used the 4MAT cycle to create an experience which focused on the conflicting themes of exploration and domination.

To transition from reflective analysis to concept development, the students were given statements that were taken directly from Christopher Columbus's log or created by Greenwood based on inferences from historical documents. Each student in a group presented one of the statements for discussion, and the group debated the expansion or domination conflict. Greenwood followed up the discussion and debate with a role-playing writing activity that moved students from historical events to their own experiences.

At Andover High School in the Bloomfield Hills School District in Farmington, Michigan, members of the Learning Style Team have proposed school-wide scheduling changes so that teachers can better accommodate student needs in their individual classrooms. According to research cited in the team's proposal, "less than 20 percent of high school students learn best through the aural channel (by listening), and approximately half of all high school students learn best if the initial contact with new and challenging concepts is through emotive/kinestic (hands-on) activities."

Mike Shelly, an Andover teacher, says the proposal calls for varying the length of class sessions, incorporating time for regular student-teacher consultations, and including common teacher planning times to allow for interdisciplinary learning. Through these and other changes, the team hopes teachers will take the opportunity to appeal to a wider range of student learning styles by implementing a greater variety of learning activities.

In the learning styles approach, it seems like the teacher assumes most of the responsibility for learning. What is the student's role?

Some critics claim teachers using a style-based approach give in to every child's whim. Advocates counter that with the learning styles approach, teachers show greater respect for diversity and place a high value on individual strengths.

High expectations do not have to be abandoned, nor do curricular and individual goals. In fact, Hodges maintains that a styles-based approach encourages students to take ownership and responsibility for learning and succeeding.

In some instances, for example, it may allow them to select the resources, setting and activities that put them most at ease; in other situations, it might spur them to stretch beyond their comfort zones and develop a fuller awareness of their own potential, as well as differences among individuals. The key, says Matthews, is that the student is actively involved and is a choice maker.

As for the teacher's role and responsibility, what seems important, most advocates say, is that he or she develops a wide range of strategies and methods to appeal to all students—within groups and as individuals. Bates, for instance, explains that with the 4MAT design, the early stages of an instructional cycle are more teacher-directed and the latter stages are more student-centered.

Prewitt has found many teachers using the style-based approach not only use a variety of strategies and methods, but they do not hesitate to employ a specific technique that appeals to an individual student's style when there is a problem. Flexibility and moving back and forth helps to build bridges while still maintaining high expectations for group and individual student achievement.

How implicit or explicit should a teacher be in the use of learning styles?

A teacher's use of the learning styles approach may be either direct and explicit; indirect, implicit; or somewhere in between. Some teachers prefer to share terms and models with their students and parents, particularly if they are using a specific instrument or inventory. Others incorporate concepts and descriptors into student feedback and activities without openly making students individually aware of specific models and their own styles.

Matthews, for example, suggests a teacher's approach may be more implicit with younger children; the child's knowledge of his or her learning style may be acquired more on an experiential rather than conceptual or verbal level. Bates, while acknowledging his approach to teaching middle school math is more implicit, knows other teachers who work with at-risk youth have found it helpful for students to understand their own style and why, perhaps, they have not been successful in more traditional classroom settings.

The crux of the issue is that students need to be aware of what makes them successful in school, and this involves style. "They need to be aware of how they learn, of traits—but not necessarily theories, concepts and jargon," says Erickson.

Adds Hodges, "One can share this information on several different levels. The teacher needs to determine what seems appropriate and relevant, and this will depend on the student and the context."

How do you balance the needs of the class as a group and the needs of the individual?

Two key words in the learning styles approach are "balance" and "acceptance." Everyone needs a time to shine. Children need to feel at ease with who they are and where they are, yet they also need to be challenged and to learn how to work within a group. Both the practitioners and the theorists are aware of the role of uncertainty and conflict in human development, relationships, and the "real world."

Many teachers using a styles-based approach build in activities that encourage students to discuss their differences so they will see there are many ways to approach a task. While these discussions take time and may be more appropriate for some lessons than for others, teachers find they provide opportunities for students to learn more than factual information—they learn about one another's thinking processes and values. In essence, they learn about other people, and this is the first step in fostering acceptance of and appreciation for diversity.

■■

Spring Cove

Understanding learning styles helped teachers in the Spring Cove School District, in Roaring Spring, Pennsylvania, eliminate pull-out instruction for all of the district's learning disabled students.

Working with the University of Pittsburgh staff, the district's coordinator for Mainstreaming Experiences for Learning Disabled trained the 30 elementary school teachers on adaptation to individual learning styles and the needs of learning disabled students. Now, the students remain in regular classes, receiving help from the special needs teacher as well as the regular classroom teacher. They meet weekly to plan lessons for co-teaching.

According to Superintendent Ivan Shibley, the MELD program also has resulted in:
• Many teachers "adapting" not only for special needs students, but also for their regular students
• Professional sharing taking place on a continuous basis
• A weekly problem-solving committee meeting that helps teachers and students adapt instruction
• A dramatic decrease in referrals for special needs.

Teachers make quick adaptations of instruction, based in part on measurements given to each student twice a week for one minute. If a student does not maintain a score on or above an established baseline, the teacher knows that adaptations of the curriculum need to be made.

■■

How do you incorporate a learning styles approach in an already established and full curriculum?

Before practitioners talk about incorporating a learning styles approach into the curriculum, they might first try to determine what they mean by the word "curriculum." Does it encompass more than content and objectives that specify what, when, and how a child should learn? Or, as Prewitt suggests, does it begin *with the child*—who she or he is, where she or he is, and what she or he needs.

Some see the approach as being congruent with some of the more progressive restructuring initiatives that attempt to move away from compartmentalizing children according to age, ability and other characteristics. Others say the learning styles approach works well within the framework of established curriculum principles. It offers teachers greater flexibility in planning lessons and activities while still striving to achieve specific outcomes and objectives.

Foriska and his staff, who have linked NASSP's conceptual styles model with specific classroom intervention activities, contend that their styles-based approach has not affected curriculum. In fact, rather than "watering down" the curriculum so more students can succeed, Foriska says he finds that when teachers use the approach, students "come up to their expectations."

Certainly, some models are more oriented to content and instructional methods for presenting information while others are more geared to the individual learner and how the student processes information. What is important, says Rita Dunn,[1] is that "students are not failing because of the curriculum. Students can learn almost any subject matter when they are taught with methods and approaches responsive to their learning style strengths. . ."

It seems as though the traditional standardized tests and group-normed student evaluations clash with the emphasis on individualized instruction in learning styles. What types of assessment might be more appropriate?

The move to style-based learning runs parallel with the need to reconsider student assessment and indicators of success. Hodges sees the whole arena of student assessment in transition. Rather than giving the same group-normed, pencil-and-paper test to everyone, researchers, practitioners, and reformists are looking for more authentic, process-oriented and open-ended ways to determine just what a student has learned.

These often include student portfolios and student-designed projects that reflect mastery, synthesis, and creative application of what the student has learned, says Prewitt. Teacher logs about student progress are another possibility. One kindergarten teacher Prewitt knew kept a note pad in her pocket and pen attached to a string around her neck so she could jot down observations as she was working with children. "It was amazing; she'd be talking with the kids and writing notes to herself at the same time," recalls Prewitt.

Staff development is critical to learning these new assessment methods, stresses Prewitt. Teachers need to develop an awareness of what is important to record, how to describe objectively what is going on, and how to give meaning to their written observations.

How might the learning styles approach be misused?

There is wide agreement among practitioners and researchers that the most potentially dangerous use of learning styles is to label and, thereby, stereotype students. Hodges believes this is a critical issue for those who attempt to link particular learning style characteristics with specific cultural or ethnic groups.

Bates and others caution that no one is ever any one style. Instead Bates sees people as a composite of different preferences and as being multimodal depending on context. For this reason, teachers need to be flexible in their application of learning style. There are times, says Bates, when a particular model is not appropriate and it might be a waste of time and energy to pursue its use. Bates also discourages teachers from choosing and using only those features they like best from any one system or approach. "If you use only part of a model, you'll get only partial success," he contends.

Another concern is that people might "lock on" to a style and use it as a crutch or an excuse, says Erickson. This applies to both students and teachers, adds Prewitt. Just as teachers have to hold students to high expectations of performance, they have to hold themselves to a high level of professional standards and conduct.

Finally, researchers and practitioners also agree that the learning styles approach is not a quick fix or cure all. "It's part of the picture, but it's not the whole picture," says Hodges.

Where is the learning styles approach and research headed?

In both practice and research, there are some tricky turns to maneuver in the future. At the practical end, there is concern about the manner in which learning styles is introduced to teachers and whether they see it as "just one more thing" being dropped on an already full plate of expectations. Many also question what type of support, in terms of long-term staff development, will be provided. Yet another rough spot is the clash over assessment methods.

At the research end, Erickson says there are concerns about the applicability of using instruments originally designed for adults with children. There are also questions about the degree of overlap across various styles, about the effectiveness of matching a particular instructional strategy to a specific style, and about the validity of research designs and alternative explanations, according to Lynn Curry.[2]

One thing seems clear, however: learning styles is not going to go away. Even though most see it as only part of the reform picture, there is a growing consensus that a style-based approach to learning complements other school reform thrusts. Some see it as providing an overarching framework for integrating cooperative learning, multicultural education, alternative forms of assessments and other initiatives. Others see it as an integral component for building parental support. Children are messengers, says Hodges, and if they are excited about school, parents will get excited, too.

The real test, say most, is the degree to which teachers, administrators, and staff members accept and respect differences among themselves and are willing to change.

■■■

What We Know About the Learning Styles Field

- Attention to learning styles research is becoming crucial because of the challenge to educate all children at high levels of performance.
- The growing diversity among students further compels an evaluation of traditional modes of instruction.
- Knowledge about the neurological characteristics of the brain provides a rich base for applying research to educational practice.
- Despite research shortcomings, the application of learning styles models and inventories to classroom practice has encouraged teachers and administrators to broaden their professional skills and offer a wider array of instructional strategies.
- Educators can anticipate a much sounder knowledge base about learning styles because of continuing research, but the lack of that base currently should not preclude exploring ways to create richer and more instructional diverse learning environments for all students.

■■■

ENDNOTES

1. Dunn, Rita, "Rita Dunn Answers Questions on Learning Styles," *Educational Leadership*, October 1990, pp. 15-19.

2. Curry, Lynn, "A Critique of the Research on Learning Styles," *Educational Leadership*, October 1990, pp. 50-52.

Acknowledgments

Learning Styles... Putting Research and Common Sense into Practice is a publication of the American Association of School Administrators, 1801 North Moore Street, Arlington, Virginia 22209-9988. AASA is the national organization for school system leaders dedicated to ensuring the highest quality of education for all learners.

The book's co-authors are Anne Lewis (Chapters 1-4) and Elizabeth Steinberger (Chapter 5). Anne Lewis is the Washington correspondent of *Phi Delta Kappan* and *Education Digest* and former editor of *Education USA*. Elizabeth Steinberger is a consultant with the McKenzie Group in Washington, D.C., and a regular contributor to AASA's *The School Administrator* magazine.

AASA extends special thanks to two individuals for sharing their expertise and insights: Helene Hodges, director of research for the Association for Supervision and Curriculum Development, Alexandria, Virginia; and James W. Keefe, director of research for the National Association of Secondary School Principals, Reston, Virginia. Appreciation also is extended to three individuals for reviewing portions of the work in progress: Christopher Harris, senior project associate with the Council of Chief State School Officers' Resource Center on Educational Equity, Washington, D.C.; Dianne Suber, principal, Dunbar Erwin Elementary School, Newport News, Virginia; and Loretta Webb, deputy superintendent, Fairfax County, Virginia, Public Schools.

Jay P. Goldman, managing editor of *The School Administrator*, served as the book's editor and managed the production, with assistance from AASA editor Leslie Eckard. AASA Associate Executive Director Gary Marx provided advice on content and served as project director. Graphics were provided by Anita Dahlman of Dahlman/Middour, McLean, Virginia.